GOOD OLD BOY

A Delta Boyhood

by WILLIE MORRIS

YOKNAPATAWPHA PRESS, INC.
Oxford, Mississippi

Some portions of this book have appeared in different form in *North Toward Home* by the same author. The author is indebted to *The Yazoo County Story*, edited by Elma Foster Nelson, for some of the raw material of Yazoo's legends. The exaggerations are all the fault of the author.

The lines on page 63 are from the song "When It's Darkness on the Delta" copyright 1932 by Stanley Bros., Inc.; renewed 1959 and assigned to World Music Inc. and Anne Rachel Music, Inc.

GOOD OLD BOY

Copyright c 1971 by Willie Morris. Renewed in 1999.

Published by Yoknapatawpha Press
P.O. Box 248, Oxford MS 38655

First published in 1971 by Harper & Row, Inc.

ISBN 0-916242-68-4

Printed in the United States of America

. . . *Be kind*
To one who cannot prove
He was a boy
By pointing to a tree, a house or creek
And saying from behind a rutted cheek,
"It was this world I was born into.
My father carried off this hill on his shoe
Into the house.
My mother swept it out."

—by Billy Edd Wheeler, mountain poet

To Omie Parker

Foreword to the 1980 Edition

When I wrote this book in 1971, I did not expect the response which came to it. I received hundreds upon hundreds of letters from children all over America. In many cases, teachers had read the book to their classes; in others, they had assigned it to their young students, or the students had come across it themselves in libraries and bookstores. I was impressed by the diversity of emotions expressed in these letters. The emotion of wonder and excitement over the small-town America of a generation or two ago seemed to predominate. Many of my young correspondents told me that the places in which they were growing up were not much different from the Yazoo of my tale. Others suggested to me their disappointment in not having had these small-town adventures. To the latter I would reply: Never mind, adventure lies deep in the heart of any young person who wishes it, just waiting there to be summoned, depending on how much you want it.

The two most frequent questions asked of me, time and again, were: where is Spit McGee now, and is everything in this book true? Spit McGee now lives, as always, far out from Yazoo in the swamplands, in a tent surrounded by twenty-six stray dogs, eighteen stray cats, six beautiful tame deer, and a pet rattlesnake. He comes to town once a month for his supplies. I ran into him on a recent trip home, buying some flour and bacon on Main Street. "That was really sumthin', what we did at the Clark Mansion that night, wasn't it?" Spit said. He confessed to me that he still wanders around that doomed mansion sometimes. Mostly Spit McGee lives close to nature under the stars and the faraway planets and takes orders from no man. He has not changed.

As for the second question—was everything in this book true?—Spit himself had found a copy and read it, and he said to me: "You told it like it was." This question in itself elicits the old and abiding things. Yes, everything in *Good Old Boy* is true, although as Mark Twain once said, sometimes you have to lie to tell the truth.

When I first wrote this book, I addressed it to my son David, who was then ten years old. Since then good old David has grown up, which somehow happens to all of us, and gone away to college. But the spirit of mischief will always reside in David, and I do not think he will mind my reprinting here the letter to him which opened the 1971 edition:

Dear David,

Last night, when we were walking your big black dog Ichabod H. Crane up Riverside Drive, you asked me what it was like when I was a boy.

You are growing up on Manhattan Island. You ride the subway and the bus by yourself all over New York City, you go to school around Columbia, and you know where Battery Park is, and the Metropolitan Museum, Grant's Tomb, the Plaza Hotel, Pennsylvania Station, Mama Leone's, Harlem, and Washington Square. You go to see the Mets, Yankees, Giants, Knicks, and Rangers play, and sometimes you have a ball game in front of your apartment house on West 94th Street.

You know all about the Dutch sailors who first came here, and you have a room of your own overlooking Broadway, with a museum of foreign coins and stamps, baseball cards from bubble-gum packs, Indian arrowheads, and old animal bones. You have even written a book, called *Dogs and Cats We Have Known*, and you like horror stories as much as I do.

You stand on the crowded street corner every night and see people of every race and color known to man go by, or you take the subway to Chinatown and eat chicken chow mein with chopsticks, or you watch the boats and barges drift by on the Hudson River. I am glad you are growing up in New York City. You say you like it because there is so much to do.

I will tell you what I was doing when I was your age: about my father; about friends of mine like Bubba Barrier and Billy Rhodes; about my many adventures and the pranks I played; about a dog I had named Old Skip. The town where I grew up in the Deep South was a very special place for me. It was different from New York City, but I hope you will never forget that my town and its people are part of what you are now. So this book, in its way, is a letter to you.

Love,
Daddy

Good Old Boy

1

Its name is Yazoo City, from the Yazoo River which
flows by it—a muddy winding stream that takes in
the Tallahatchie, the Sunflower, and countless other
smaller creeks and rivers before it finally empties itself into the Mississippi a few miles north of Vicksburg. "Yazoo," far from being the funny name that
many think it, always meant something a little dark
and crazy for me. It is an old Indian name that
means "Death" or "Waters of the Dead," for the Indians who once lived here as fighters and hunters had
died of some strange and dreadful disease. Stephen
Foster at first meant his song to be "Way Down Upon
the Yazoo River," but he found out about the mean-
ing of the word and felt he had been tricked. Years
later when I left to go to college, I was called "Yazoo"
—such was the spell the very name had on you long
after you had left it, for its people have always been
given to somber fancies and the most peculiar fears
and hallucinations. It is a land of lingering orange
twilights that cast a burnt glow, old as time itself; of

sudden storms that bend the prodigious trees into anguished shapes; of smoky afternoons where the cry of a mysterious swamp bird or the sound of an axe on wood carries for miles and miles around. Little wonder that this dark country has shaped its people in its own brooding image, or that strange and memorable things have happened there to the boys who grew up in it.

The town sits there crazily, half on the green hills and half on the delta. Once, many thousands of years ago, this flat delta land was the very floor of the sea. Later it was covered with great swampy forests, and any person who wandered into them by himself would get very lonely and afraid; he would have to be wary of the quicksand, not to mention the giant lizards, snakes, alligators, spiders, and Indians. Now it is the richest land in the world. Some say if you plant a cotton seed in it, you have to jump away quickly to avoid being hit by the growing stalk.

For a boy growing up in the 1940s it was a pleasant old town. Some of its streets were not paved, although most of them would be after a time. The main street, stretching its several blocks from the Dixie Theater down to the bend in the river, was always narrow and dingy. But down along the quiet, shady streets, with their pecan and magnolia and elm and locust trees, were the stately old houses that had been built long before the Civil War.

All this was before they built the big supermarkets and shopping centers. It was even before there was television, and people would not close their doors and shut their curtains to watch the quiz games and the Western gun fights. They would sit out on their front porches in the hot quiet nights and say hello to everyone who walked by. If the fire truck came past, they all got in their cars to follow it. The houses were set out in a line under the soft green trees, their leaves rustling gently with the breeze. The broad lawns would be wet with a summer's dew, the lightning bugs glowed and vanished as far as the eye could see, and the night would be alive with the rumbling and chirping of small delta things. Suddenly there would be the roar of the eight o'clock Illinois Central on its Memphis-to-New Orleans run, a brief violent interlude that gave way to a sad little echo down the railroad track. It was a lazy town, stretched out on its hills and its flat streets in a summer sun; a dreamy place, always green and lush except for the four cold months at the beginning and end of each year. It was heavy with leafy smells, and in springtime there was a perfume in the air that made you dizzy if you breathed in too much of it. At night it was full of noises and lost ghosts—the witch in the cemetery who burned down the whole town in 1904, the giant-sized Indians buried in the Indian mounds which had been leveled to build the town, Casey Jones crashing into the freight train a few miles down the road, the Yankees in the gunboat that had sunk in the River during the Civil War.

Many years ago, there was an exceptionally mean and ugly woman who lived alone, in carefully guarded seclusion, near the banks of the Yazoo River. Nobody knew anything about her, but they loathed her nonetheless. They hated her so much they didn't even give her a name. It was rumored that on stormy nights she would lure fishermen into her house, poison them with arsenic, and bury them on a densely wooded hill nearby. This was her hobby, but although many people suspected her of these evil diversions, no one was able to prove anything. Then one late afternoon in the autumn of 1884, a boy named Joe Bob Duggett was passing by her house on a raft when he heard a terrible, ungodly moan from one of the rooms. He tied his raft to a cypress branch, ran to the house, and looked through a window. What he saw chilled his blood and bones. Two dead men were stretched out on the floor of the parlor, and the old woman, wearing a black dress caked with filth and cockleburs, had turned her face up to the ceiling and was singing some dreadful incantation, waving her arms in demented circles all the while.

Joe Bob Duggett raced to his raft, floated into town, and told the sheriff and his men what he had seen. They got a horse and buggy and sped to the old woman's house. They smashed down the front door, but were unable to find either the dead men (who have never been found to this day) or the demented old woman. They climbed the stairs to the attic, opened the door an inch or two, and caught sight of several dozen half-starved cats, all bunched together and gyrating in their wild insanity. Two skeletons, which were never identified by the sheriff's office, dangled from a dusty rafter. Fish bones littered the floor, and the smell was unusually pungent. The sheriff, his deputies, and Joe Bob stood there transfixed, finally banging the door shut when eight or ten of the cats tried to get out.

Then from the backyard they heard the sound of footsteps in the fallen pecan leaves, and from an upstairs window they saw the old woman sneaking away into the swamps which abounded along the River. "Stop in the name of the law!" the sheriff shouted, but the old woman, who, as Joe Bob Duggett would later tell his grandchildren, looked "half ghost and half scarecrow, but *all* witch," took off into the swamps at a maniacal gallop. They followed in hot pursuit, and a few minutes later they came upon a sight that Joe Bob remembered so well he would describe it again, for the thousandth time, on his deathbed in the King's Daughters Hospital in 1942. The old woman had been trapped in a patch of quicksand, and they caught up with her just seconds before her ghastly, pockmarked head was about to go under. But she had time to shout these words at her pursuers: *I shall return. Everybody always hated me here. I will break out of my grave and burn down the whole town on the morning of May 25, 1904!* Then, as Joe Bob also described it later, with a gurgle and a retch the woman sank from sight to her just desserts.

With the aid of pitchforks and long cypress limbs the authorities were able to retrieve her body. The next day, with the wind and rain sweeping down from the hills, they buried her in the center of the town cemetery, in a cluster of trees and bushes, and around her grave they put the heaviest chain they could find—some thirty strong and solid links. "If she can break through *that* and burn down Yazoo," the sheriff said, more in fun than seriously, "she deserves to burn it down."

The years went by, the long Mississippi seasons came and went, and the town forgot the old woman.

On the morning of May 25, 1904, some twenty years later, Miss Pauline Wise was planning her wedding. As she entered her parlor to show her visitor some gifts, she discovered a small blaze. Suddenly a strong wind, unusual for that time of year, spread the fire to the adjoining house. From Main Street the fire spread to all intersecting streets and soon reached the residential section. The roar of the ever-increasing flames, the confusion of terrorized thousands, the hoarse shouts of the firefighters, and the sound of crashing walls made a scene of awesome horror that remained a fixed picture in the memory of eyewitnesses as long as their lives lasted Many fine homes were destroyed, and every bank, every physician's, lawyer's and dentist's office, every hotel and boardinghouse, every meat market and bakery, the newspaper and printing office, every church, club room, and lodge room, every telephone, telegraph and express office, the depot, the post office, every furniture store, every hardware store, all but one livery stable, all but one drugstore, every barbershop, every tailor shop, every undertaking establishment, and, in fact, nearly every business necessity.

The next day, after the murderous flames had consumed themselves, several elder citizens of the town made a journey to the grave in the middle of the cemetery. What they discovered would be passed along to my friends and to me many years later, and as boys we would go see it for ourselves, for no repairs were made, as a reminder to future generations. As if by some supernatural strength, *the chain around the grave had been broken in two.*

This immense and grievous tale alone would have been enough to make us woefully mortal Yazoo boys susceptible to the ghostly presences in our midst as we grew up in the 1940s. But on still, cold nights in the fall, as the mists whirled and eddied out of the delta, and the wind whistling and moaning from the woods made our hearts pound in fear and excitement, we had other things to remind us that this was unusual country to have been born in. *For the town itself had been built on a graveyard.* When the first settlers moved into the countryside that later was to become the town, they discovered two massive and solitary Indian mounds, each with a diameter of almost four hundred feet and a height of more than fifty.

When these mounds were leveled to make way for streets, they were found to contain bowls, weapons, and other artifacts of a civilization unlike that of any known Indians. The grave vaults themselves were twelve feet long, but there was no sign of skeletons—only ashes. None of the Indians alive at the time knew about this vanished race, although Choctaw tradition spoke of a race of giants: a savage tribe of tattooed warriors eight or nine feet tall who roamed the swamps and the woods terrorizing both man and beast. On rainy nights during the equinox, the first settlers were said to have heard the muffled tread of footsteps in the mud. It is too bad that Joe Bob Duggett was not alive in those olden days to pursue these curious vibrations; but what boy would have been so lion-hearted and intrepid? Certainly not I. Any boy, knowing about the legends of the race of red giants and finding himself alone after sundown near the place of those ancient graves, would have been foolhardy not to quicken his steps and set out for the comforting lights of Main Street.

Of considerably more inspiration to the boys of Yazoo in the 1940s was the legend of Casey Jones. Casey and his fireman, Sim Webb, on engine No. 382 of the Illinois Central Railroad, were assigned to the Cannonball Express run on the morning of April 30, 1900. Everyone in the countryside recognized Casey's engine because it was equipped with his own special whistle, a calliope that echoed across vast distances. Those who heard its eerie sound were often frightened out of sleep by it, but it was Casey Jones' own private trademark, and on this night many years ago it was a harbinger of death and unique heroism.

The countryside knew by the whistle's moans
That the man at the throttle was Casey Jones.

Shortly after Casey's train entered Yazoo County, just a few miles outside of town, he looked far down the tracks and sighted the caboose of another train jutting out on the main line. Casey was going too fast to stop in time, but he stayed with his engine, managing to slow his speeding train just enough to save the lives of his passengers and crew. Sim Webb followed Casey's orders and jumped only moments before No. 382 plummeted into the caboose, but Casey Jones was killed instantly.

Casey's story survived to inspire our imagination, for in truth our imagination required constant stoking—much like a coal fire on an Illinois Central engine. Nearly fifty years after that fateful night, Bubba Barrier, Muttonhead Shepherd, and I, driving along the railroad tracks in Bubba's red Model A Ford, stopped at a house to ask for a drink of water. For an hour the owner entertained us with stories of Casey Jones, who had been a friend of his; then he went into a back room and brought out a large bell. It was the bell from Casey Jones' locomotive! Good old Bubba offered the man his Model A Ford for that bell, but the offer was not accepted.

And finally, among the many stories that haunted our dreams, the Yankee gunboat lying at the bottom of the Yazoo River near the old sawmill occupied a place of high priority. All during the Civil War, that most wonderful of adventures which it had been our ill luck to miss, the Yankee boats steamed up the Yazoo from Vicksburg to lob a few shells into town, just to remind the townspeople who was boss. One afternoon in 1863 the Confederates fired back, sinking the intruder and every damn Yankee on board.

That unfortunate boat remained at the bottom for years, a reminder of all the deprivation and heroism of those tragic days. Billy Rhodes and Muttonhead Shepherd, out catfishing one night in a rowboat, saw an unearthly green glow deep down in the waters, and heard voices crying for help in alien Yankee accents. Big Boy Wilkinson and Henjie Henick were throwing rocks at turtles near the same spot six months later and heard the strains of a song that sounded ominously like "The Battle Hymn of the Republic." Peewee Baskin thought he had a goggle-eye on his fish hook two years after that, and he pulled out a saucer with the likeness of a man in a beard and stovepipe hat stamped on it. If we had not beaten the Yankees, Peewee surmised, that rusty old boat might emerge from the waters all of a sudden someday and demand that Yazoo surrender.

Finally, many years later, a salvage crew came to town and, after weeks of strenuous labor, brought the gunboat to the surface. They found skeletons, perfectly good ink in several inkwells, and food that was still stuck to the plates.

When I was six months old, my mother and father moved the forty miles from Jackson to Yazoo. My mother cried over leaving the big city for such a small country town. People were still talking about the Great Flood of 1927. The Mississippi River had broken out of its levees that year, and the water had reached the houses on the street where we were to live. There were watermarks on the walls of the older houses. In one vacant field the water moccasins had been so thick they were wrapped around each other; there had been carcasses of horses and cows, and floating dogs and telephone poles. Even the Yazoo River played tricks on the town, coming out of its banks almost every spring to flood part of the business section and leave the streets and roads covered in ooze and filth sent down to us from Minnesota, Illinois, and Missouri.

At first we lived in a small frame house with a front porch shaded by great oak trees, next door to a girl who carried me around on her back and would one day be Miss Mississippi and runner-up for Miss America. We lived with "Aunt Tish," not our aunt at all but an ancient old lady almost 90 years old whom everyone, in the Southern manner of that day, called "Aunt." It is Aunt Tish whom my uncertain memory tells me I saw first. Back in some old mist a swing broke and crashed to the floor, and an old lady picked me up and began humming a tune. The night was still except for the katydids around, singing "katy-did, katydidn't, katydid, katydidn't," and for some reason I chose that moment to take notice of this planet.

I remember the cold, quiet nights and the stifling hot summers, starched summer suits and the smell of talcum, sweet-smelling black people in white dresses—my "nurses," who could be adoring and gentle and then impatient and rough—tugs at my hand and a high rich voice telling me, "If you don't behave, boy, the police gonna put you *under* the jail." There were three big birddogs named Tony, Sam, and Jimbo, their warm licks and loud barks, the feel of their bodies against mine in front of a black stove, the way they bounded into my bed to get me out to play, the taste of gingerbread and hot corn on the cob, and my whispered words, "God bless everybody and me." God blessed, with affection and comfort, three birddogs and the little girl next door.

My father had a huge green truck—so large I had to sit on a box to see out of its windows—and from the back came the heady smell of gasoline, which my father sold to make a living. There was a gas station to play in and, somewhere down a wide street and beyond a railroad track, a place with tanks, plat-forms to jump from, a cool warehouse with dirt for a floor, and room for the dogs to run and bark in the tall grass on a hill. Later we moved down Grand Ave-nue to our own house, set in a big yard with walnut, elm, and pecan trees.

One day the grass and weeds in the backyard caught fire. A Negro man walking down the street saw the fire and ran to help. We fought it with blankets and water. Then, when we had put out the fire, I ran to the dresser where I kept all my pennies, and rushed out and caught up with the man and gave them to him.

My mother played the pipe organ in the Methodist Church. Sometimes, early on Sunday mornings, I would go listen to her while she practiced under a beautiful stained-glass window. I remember the hymns she played: "Abide With Me," "Bringing in the Sheaves," "Rock of Ages." The music drifted through the empty church and made me drowsy, and I would stretch out under a pew and fall fast asleep. She also taught children to play the piano. It was a large black grand piano which took up almost half the space in our front room, and on late afternoons when it began to get dark I would sit in my room and listen to the music from the front. It was not the music they played over and over, up and down the scale, that I liked, but the songs my mother played when she told the children, "Now *I'll* play your piece all the way through like Mr. Mozart would want it played." I can sometimes hear her music now, after thirty years, and remember the leaves falling on some smoky autumn afternoon, the air crisp and the sounds of dogs barking and train whistles far away.

2

When I was five my mother took me by the hand into the two-story brick schoolhouse on Main Street, and left me in the care of Miss Bass, a stern old lady who looked as if she would bite. Bubba Barrier was in my room. Someone was supposed to get me after the first day was out, but failed to come. Bubba and I were frightened, but finally we walked hand in hand away from the school, along the bayou, up Grand Avenue and home. Such adventure befitted a boy's stature as a first grader in the Free Public School System of Yazoo County, Mississippi.

The school was a big old structure with white columns, iron fire escapes, and tall old-fashioned windows. It was set in a large plot of three or four acres; the public library was at one end of the lot, and at the other, in the farthest corner of the grounds, the gray Confederate monument. On top of the monument about thirty feet from the ground were two statues: a lady holding a Confederate flag in front of her, and a soldier with a rifle in one hand, his other hand slightly raised to accept the flag—but a little shyly, as if he did not want to go around all day holding both a flag and a gun, particularly with a ten-inch bayonet attached.

Inside, the school building was all long, shadowy halls, smelling always of wax. On the wall near the front door were portraits of George Washington and Jefferson Davis. Downstairs was a large basement, where we met to wait for the morning bell to ring on rainy days and where, at noon, we took our lunch. It was a dark, eerie place; I was to have a nightmare of those years. I am trying to climb out of the sunless basement through a small, narrow window to the playground outside. The window is not big enough. My trouser legs are caught in it, nothing can budge me. The bell rings, everyone goes upstairs, and I am left alone. Some rainy gray mornings, waiting in that concrete chamber with its one light bulb in the peeled ceiling casting strange shadows, I could hardly bear the time until the bell rang. The room was attached to the boys' toilet, and from it came the echoes of the toilets flushing. Off to the side, in a kind of wired-in room, was the lunch hall, where lunches sold for a dime apiece and where the teachers, with shouts and sometimes slaps, would make us finish all our wieners and sauerkraut or bologna and black-eyed peas. It was our small contribution to the "war effort," eating everything on our plate. It might have been easier to lose the war.

All this was in the early 1940s, and the Second

World War was on to defend democracy, as our teachers told us. They told us we were in school to help democracy, to strengthen our country and our God, and to learn enough so we could make good money for ourselves. In the assembly hall upstairs, where we marched in every Friday with the music teacher playing the March from *Aida* on the spinet piano, the American flag on the right of the stage and the Confederate flag on the left, the speaker would tell us of the man he once knew who could have been President of the United States, except that when the time came for him to be chosen, some of his friends felt honorbound to tell everybody that he had been lazy, lied a great deal, and had taken to liquor when he was young; so he never got the chance to be President. Quite frankly, I did not believe this story, and neither did Bubba Barrier.

I had a friend named Spit McGee who lived far out in the country. Spit was something of a lone wolf. He wore khaki clothes and did not come to school except when the mood was upon him. He was long and skinny, with a red face and a nose that should have belonged with somebody else's face. His given name was Clarence, but he concealed that fact; he could spit farther than anyone else, and with unusual accuracy.

Spit lived in the swamps, and he was a hunter and fisherman. Foxie Tompkins might bring an apple to school for the teacher, but not Spit. If he brought her anything it would be a catfish, or a dead squirrel for frying. Rivers Applewhite was often the recipient of the most beautiful wild swamp flowers, which Spit brought into town in the spring. One day he brought the teacher a dead chicken snake in a burlap sack, and a chicken was still inside the snake's belly (or whatever snakes call bellies); but the teacher made him bury it behind the Confederate monument. Later she caught him chewing tobacco near the snake's grave and gave him an F in Conduct. When she caught him smoking a Camel two weeks later she sent a note to Spit's mother, but Spit told me he wasn't worried because his mother couldn't read.

One day during recess Spit reached into his pockets and pulled out a dead grubworm, a live boll weevil, a wad of chewed-up bubble gum, four leaves of poison ivy which he said he was not allergic to, two shotgun shells, a small turtle, a rusty fish hook, the feather from a wild turkey, a minnow, the shrunken head of a chipmunk, and a slice of bacon. Spit may not have been smart in the ways of books, but he was diligent and resourceful, with a wisdom that came straight from the swamps. He claimed that he had taken an old useless .12 gauge shotgun and made it into a pellet gun, manufacturing his own bullets from rusty tin cans and soaking them in a mixture of frog's blood, burnt moss, dust from rattlesnake rattles, cypress juice, and mashed black widow spiders. When a victim was hit by one of these pellets, he said, it would not kill him, but knock him completely unconscious for three hours. He even said he had tried it once on his father, who was drunk in a willow tree, and that his father, not knowing what hit him, had not only been knocked out for six hours but once he did awaken gave up whiskey for three months.

We were envious of him not merely because of the bounty he carried in his pockets, but because he came to school barefooted whenever he felt like it, while we had to wear shoes that pinched our big toes and made our feet itch. He also claimed he could predict when it would rain from an ache he got in his arm, which he had broken falling out of a china-berry tree. To my knowledge he was not wrong on a single rainfall. He further claimed that he was the great-great-nephew of Joe Bob Duggett—the boy who had discovered the witch in 1884—that he had once spent the night sleeping on an old blanket on the witch's grave in the cemetery, that he had dug up a grave in a Baptist cemetery on a plantation near the River, and that he had not taken a bath since the previous Easter. On the first three points we felt he was lying, but we believed him on the fourth.

At noon recess one day, when we were in third grade, Spit said he was going to play a prank on our teacher. Then he took off mysteriously for the bayou with a big box under his arm. When the bell rang half an hour later and we filed into our room, I saw a sight such as I will never forget. About three dozen crawdads, in all postures and movements, were crawling around the room. Five or six of them were on the teacher's desk, and one had gotten into her purse. The teacher was in a state of considerable anger, and she demanded to know who had done this horrible deed. For a while there was silence, and then Foxie Tompkins and Edith Stillwater, the teacher's pets, shouted almost at once. "It was Spit McGee!" Poor Spit got three paddlings: one from the teacher, one from the principal, and one from the superintendent of city schools, the last one being the worst because the superintendent had a paddle with air holes in it to make bigger blisters.

The next day there was revenge on a massive scale. Since I had taken Edith Stillwater to two war movies at the Dixie Theater (*Guadalcanal Diary* and *Flying Leathernecks*), spending ten cents each on her, I demanded the return of my twenty cents. (She only gave me back a dime.) She was giving a piano recital at the Baptist Church that afternoon before about fifty proud and cooing relatives and friends; we sneaked into the church early and got the piano out of tune, scraped some fresh cow manure onto the piano pedals, and placed a stray alley cat inside the piano and put the top back down. Then, led by Spit, we cornered Foxie Tompkins and marched him off to our official meeting place, the chicken shed behind Henjie Henick's house. After borrowing a rope from Henjie, Spit tied one end to the rafter and made a hangman's noose with the other. Then we put Foxie on a wooden box, tightened the noose around his neck, and told him to apologize fifty times in a row, but that he had better do it quickly because the box was shaky and if it fell over, that would be the end of Foxie's fine career, both in school and otherwise. We retired from the chicken coop and closed the door. From outside we heard Foxie apologizing rapidly, in a determined but squeaky voice. Just at that moment a funeral came by on Grand Avenue, and we went over to watch it. We forgot about Foxie. Luckily for his career, Henjie Henick's mother went back to feed the chickens and found Foxie balancing on his toes just as the box was beginning to fall over.

At the Baptist Church, we were told later, the cat squealed as Edith Stillwater started her off-key étude, ruining the recital. All that remained was to take the crawdads, which the teacher had returned to Spit, back to the bayou. As a celebration, Spit led us to the chicken snake's grave and we dug it up, to find that the snake had rotted but the chicken was still there.

This list of my schooltime favorites, Bubba, Spit, and all the rest, would not be complete without the one I think of the most: Rivers. Rivers Applewhite. She was without doubt the most beautiful girl in our class, but she was not a demure kind of beauty. Not at all. She wore her dark brown hair short (sometimes the way the models did in *Harper's Bazaar*) to offset her fine willowy grace, and she had deep green eyes, and in spring and summer she was always brown as a berry from all the time she spent in the sun. I am also pleased to say that she was not a tomboy; who in his proper senses would want a girl to kick a football farther than he could, or out-run him in the 50-yard dash? She was smart as could be—much smarter than Edith Stillwater, even though Edith got better grades—and she got Spit McGee through final exams in the third grade by bribing him, with the lemon pies she always was baking, to practice his long division and memorize poems. (Spit McGee once recited Browning: "Oh to be in April, Now that England's here.") She was also partial to Old Skip, my dog, and would bring him bones and cotton candy, so Skip was a regular old fool over Rivers Applewhite, sidling up to her with his tail wagging, putting his wet black nose against the palm of her hand, jumping and gyrating in her presence like the craziest creature alive. Unlike some of the other girls, especially Edith Stillwater, she would never so much as consider telling the teacher on anybody, and to this day I cannot recall a traitor-ous or deceitful act on her part.* Kind, beautiful, a fount of good fun and cheer, she was the best of all feminine symbols to the wild and unregenerate boys of Yazoo. All of us, dogs and boys alike, were a little

* In later life Rivers married a prominent young United States Senator from a border state. I hope, as some newspaper columnists now believe, that someday she will be the First Lady of the Land. Edith Stillwater is a biophysicist and a leader of Women's Liberation in Ann Arbor, Michigan.

bit in love with Rivers Applewhite.

I remember her in a white summer dress, one day shortly before Christmas in Yazoo, walking up a sidewalk of Main Street under the bright holiday tinsel. As always, we were riding in Bubba's old red Ford, and we saw her from half a block away, recognizing her from behind by the way she walked, half on her toes and half on her heels. As we got up close behind her near Kuhn's Nickel and Dime Store, I noticed that she *rippled* along that sidewalk, and that when she passed by people coming her way, just smiling calmly and being her jaunty self, they got a smile on their faces too.

There was terror for me in that school. Miss Abbott was my fourth grade teacher, and for the first time my grades were bad and my conduct report worse.

Miss Abbott had a pink nose and came from a small town in South Mississippi. The only book she ever read through and through, she told us, was the Bible, and you lived to believe her, and to feel bad about the day she got hold of that book. I myself liked the Bible. I had my own private friendship with God, which included the good old hymns and quiet mumbled prayers and holy vengeance when it was really deserved, and in that town and in that age you took God so much for granted that you knew he was keeping a separate book on you as part of His day's work.

But Miss Abbott's religion was one of fear and terror—it got you by the hind end and never let go. It was a thing of long, crazy speeches; she wanted you to believe she herself was in telephone contact with the Lord, and had hung the moon for Him on day number four. She played a little plastic flute which she had bought at Woolworth's for a quarter, and she would play us rousing hymns and marches, paying no attention to the saliva trickling down the instrument to the floor. She would not drink Coca-Cola, she said, because of the liquor hidden in it. She would preach to us every day: if God ever caught us doing something wrong, she said, we would surely go to hell before the next sunrise.

Twice a day, early in the morning and in the afternoon after lunch, she would call on each of us to pray. We would all begin by blessing our soldiers and then ripping into the Germans and the Japs. Once Spit began his prayer by saying, "Dear Lord, thank you for the bombs that ain't fallin' on us," and then stopped. "What's wrong?" the teacher asked, and he said, "I just can't think of nuthin' else to say." Then would come the Bible verses. For two hours each morning she would make us recite the verses she had assigned us to learn by heart. When we forgot a verse, she would rap our palms with a twelve-inch ruler. Then out would come that flute again, and if she caught you drowsing while she piped away on some song, or scratching your weary tail, she would go to her conduct book, and with a slight little flourish write down a "5."

I made the mistake of correcting her one day, during one of the rare hours in which we were doing schoolwork. The capital of Missouri, she said, was St. Louis. I held up my hand.

"What is it, Willie?" she asked.

"Miss Abbott, the capital of Missouri is Jefferson City."

"No, it's St. Louis."

"I bet it's Jefferson City," I said, and then immediately wished I hadn't said it because the Bible was against gambling.

"Kay King," she snapped, "look in the book and show him it's St. Louis."

The girl looked in the book and turned red. "Well," she said, "it says here Jefferson City," but frightened, like everyone else in that ill-fated class, she added, "But Miss Abbott ought to—"

"We'll see," Miss Abbott growled, and changed the subject. Later, during "silent study," I caught her glowering at me. Why couldn't those wretched people in Missouri have settled on St. Louis? Then Rivers Applewhite sent a note over to me that said: "I'm proud of you. Someday you will be Governor of Mississippi."

At noon recess that spring, while the teacher sat on the grass with a group of fawning little girls around her who fetched things for her and scratched her back when it itched, gave her little compliments and practiced their Bible verses, held her hand and looked for four-leaf clovers to put behind her red ears, we were playing softball nearby. Honest Ed Upton hit a lazy foul that went high into the air behind third base. From shortstop I watched it come down with mounting interest, with an almost fanatic regard, as the ball drifted earthward and smacked Miss Abbott on the head. She sprawled on the ground, with a moo like a milk cow's—out cold. *Oh joy of joys!* The other teachers picked her up and carried her away in a car. In our room later, with the principal looking out for us, all the little girls cried—silent little bawls—and even Honest Ed Upton shed tears. The boys scratched their heads and fiddled with their pencils; such was the fear in that room, they dared not look into one another's eyes. All except Spit McGee. He caught a glance of mine and puckered up his lips, and before long a note in pencil came over from him—*i wich she got hit with a hardbal insted.* I prayed that she would die.

But back she came, risen on the third day. One Friday afternoon, when she had stepped out of the room, I made a spitball and threw it over two rows at Kay King. *"Willie!"* The sound of Miss Abbott's voice sent terror to my soul. Each afternoon during that wonderful spring I had to stay in, two hours a day for six weeks, working long division. Miss Abbott would sit at her desk, reading the Bible or *Reader's Digest,* while the shadows got longer and the sound of the boys' voices wafted in through the open window. And when that year ended, with a C on my report card in math, I had crossed, waded, swum the Sea of Galilee, and joyously entered the city limits of old Jerusalem.

3

My early school years were not all divine unhappiness. There were trips in the late afternoons to the town library, a cool and private place, where I would sit in a quiet corner and read the latest serials in *Boys' Life* or *Open Road for Boys*, or examine the long rows of books and wonder what was in them and why they were there. Or I would go down to the *Yazoo Herald* on Wednesday nights and watch them put out the weekly newspaper; the people who owned it would invite me in and let me examine the long lead galleys of type, and the noisy clattering linotype machines. Sunday mornings I would go to town with my father to buy the comics. In the early stillness, with almost no one stirring, I would walk right down the center of Main Street as if I owned it all myself.

One day in the library I found an old book about the town. It had photographs of Main Street taken many years before, crowded with horses and buggies and people in outrageous clothes; I pored over those pictures, with all their comings and goings of people long since dead. There was a picture of an old man under an oak tree behind our schoolhouse, and I recognized the tree! I was so delighted by this discovery that I went outside and walked over to the tree; it was at least three times bigger than it was in the old photograph. I stood where the old man had stood, on the precise spot, and I wondered who the old man was. I knew surely he must be dead. The whole business, the tree and the old man, made me feel a little dizzy, but I felt I had learned something I had not known before. I went back to the book in the library, and I looked at photographs of little boys and girls of 75 years ago, in front of other trees and buildings I knew, and looking at their faces I saw the faces of their grandsons and granddaughters, who were my friends. *Why, this old town,* I thought to myself, *it seems to bind everything up.*

My friends were good old boys, and good old boys never let you down. They were Bubba, Billy Rhodes, Honest Ed, Muttonhead, Ralph, Peewee, The Cat, Henjie, Big Boy, Strawberry, Moosie, Loud Mouth Buddy, Van Jon, and Spit (when he was in school).

Here is an official roster I once compiled for a football game with boys from another town.

With the exception of our girl friend, Rivers Applewhite, we did not like girls as much as we liked dogs, cats, bugs, rabbits, turtles, and fish. Some

NAME	NICK-NAME	HEIGHT	WEIGHT	FATHER'S OCCUPATION
Alias, Ellis	Strawberry	50"	90	merchant
Atkinson, Ralph	(none)	56"	79	insurance man
Barrier, Hilary	Bubba	55"	80	planter
Baskin, Marion	Peewee	49"	60	planter
Henick, Wilson	Henjie	60"	60	tire salesman
McGee, Clarence	Spit	58"	83	unknown
Moorhead, Doyle	Moosie	54"	62	doctor
Morris, Skipper	Old Skip	18"	30	hunting dog
Morris, William	Willie	56"	73	Cities Service station
Pugh, Robert	The Cat	59"	78	merchant
Rhodes, Dusty	(none)	36"	39	father unknown
Rhodes, William	Billy	49"	65	car salesman
Russell, Frank	Loud Mouth Buddy	56"	71	truck driver
Shepherd, Bill	Muttonhead	55"	79	merchant
Upton, Edwin	Honest Ed	59"	60	Texaco station
Ward, Van Jon	(none)	54"	70	merchant
Wilkinson, Charles	Big Boy	61"	90	policeman

afternoons we would go to the cotton gin, a sprawling tin building with cotton bales piled almost to the roof—a perfect place for hiding and climbing. Or we would take long rambling hikes up to Peak Teneriffe on the old valley road, which once was an Indian trail, and stand high on the bluffs and look out over the great delta, flat, dark, and unbroken as far as you could see, with not a hill or rise from that spot to Memphis, 180 miles away. Or we would walk up the bayou, which had been dug deep into the earth to bring the waters down, two miles or more, from Brickyard Hill and the cemetery, through the residential section, past the cotton gin and on into the Yazoo River. At certain times of the year, when the water was coming out of the hills, the bayou would be crawling with hundreds of crawdads. We would walk under one bridge after another, following the source of the water until the bayou itself ran out, and then on into the hills where the Negro shacks were, coming back only when the lights of the town began to twinkle far below.

And the coming of the spring in that old town! Even today it is an echo in the heart: the wild rustling of the land, which hummed like a living being; the overpowering fragrances of the berries, vines, flowers, and grasses; the unceasing song of the katydids in the wild and magic nighttime: this was time for a boy to crave any adventure the Lord might place before him, and time for a craving in the soul that even the boy himself did not understand.

In the spring and summer we would go to the political rallies in some vast and dusty clearing in the middle of the woods. The barbecue and sweet potatoes and corn on the cob and biscuits were stacked on long tables and served up by country people. We would sit on the grass with this steaming feast in our laps, lazily eating and listening to the preachers and the politicians. Once Pearl Hanna, a shriveled old lady who rode in a black carriage and got her name from the pearl-handled pistols which she always wore at her side, got up to announce her candidacy for sheriff of Yazoo County. She said, "My platform ain't but one thing, and that's to clean up the jail. If you ain't never been in there you should. It's a mess, the floors ain't been swept and the toilets ain't flushed. I intend to get it cleaned out or die tryin'."

Peewee Baskin's father had a plantation out beyond the River. One afternoon Bubba Barrier, Ralph Atkinson, and I went out to help Peewee clean out his barn. After a time Spit McGee appeared from nowhere. He had been wandering in the woods, and he came up to the barn carrying two dead squirrels by their tails. Later all of us got on Peewee's mules and started riding down the gravel road toward the River. No one was armed except Bubba, who was carrying a BB gun. I was on the mule next to Bubba's.

All of a sudden there was a loud bang, and I felt a sharp pain in my neck. I reached up and felt it, and there was a BB lodged about an eighth of an inch into my neck. It hurt.

"Bubba!" I shouted, "you just shot me in the neck with your BB gun!" I picked the BB out and threw it angrily on the road.

"I did not!" Bubba said.

"You did so too," I said.

"I did so not!" Bubba shouted back. He was getting mad.

"I think you did, Bubba," Peewee interjected. "You're the only one with a BB gun."

"Even if it was an accident," Ralph said, "I think it was your gun."

"It still wasn't me," Bubba said.

Spit had been spitting tobacco on his mule's ear. "It wasn't Bubba that done it," Spit said, speaking with deliberation. "It was the gun. The ol' gun done it all by hisself."

To this day I have a scar on my neck from Bubba's BB gun. Elsewhere, I have a scar on my ankle from the time Spit McGee and Strawberry Alias tackled me in a football game and knocked me up against the water hydrant; a scar on my left elbow from falling off the Confederate monument; a scar on my thigh from cutting myself on a Nehi Strawberry Soda bottle in Henjie Henick's chicken shed; a scar on the top of my head from when Big Boy Wilkinson hit me with a horseshoe; and a scar on my right hand where at a picnic Billy Rhodes threw a glowing coal with a pair of tongs when I wasn't looking and shouted "Catch!" My whole body from head to toe is a repository and testimony to these old years in Yazoo.

My body got its scars, and I learned these things:

1. *I did not like to sit still.*
2. *My tail would start itching ten minutes after a preacher started a sermon.*
3. *Rattlesnakes were not to be meddled with when they were looking at you.*
4. *Adults would never believe you when you believed something very strongly.*

32

5. *Speakers who came to talk to our school assembly did not believe what they said—either that or they were bigger fools than they seemed.*
6. *I was getting smarter than my father all the time.*

4

One day during my imprisonment under Miss Abbott I got Old Skip, the best dog I ever owned, shipped from a kennel all the way from Springfield, Missouri. He was a black-and-white fox terrier. I had never been without a dog for more than six months at a time; this one had been promised to me ever since I behaved myself at my first funeral.

I came across a faded photograph of him not too long ago, his black face with the long nose sniffing at something in the air, his tail straight and pointing, his eyes flashing with mischief. Looking at a photograph taken a quarter of a century before, I admit that even as a grown man I still miss him. We had had a whole string of dogs before, first big birddogs like Tony, Sam, and Jimbo, and then purebred English smooth-haired fox terriers like this one. I got to know all about dogs—their crazy moods, how they looked when they were sick or just bored, when they were ready to bite or when their growling meant nothing, what they might be trying to say when they moaned and made strange human noises deep in their throats.

None of those other dogs could compare with this one. You could talk to him as well as you could to some human beings, and he would understand more of what you said than some people I knew. He would look you straight in the eye, and when he knew what you were saying he would turn his head sideways, back and forth, his ears cocked to get every word. Before going to bed at night I would say, "First thing tomorrow I want you to get your leash, and then come get me up, 'cause we're gonna get in the car and go out in the woods and get us some *squirrels*." And the next morning he would wake up both my father and me, get the leash, walk nervously around the house while we ate breakfast, and then lead us out to the car. Or I could say, "Bubba Barrier and Billy Rhodes are comin' over here today, and we're gonna play some football." And his face would light up, and he would wait around in front of the house and pick up Bubba's and Billy Rhodes' scent a block down the street and come tell me they were coming. Or, "Skip, how about some catch?" and he would get up and walk into the front room, open the door in the cabinet with his long nose, and bring me the tennis ball.

Every time I shouted "*Squirrel!*" Skip would head for the nearest tree and try to climb it, sometimes getting as high as five or six feet with his spectacular leaps. This would stop traffic on the street in front of our house. People in cars would see him trying to climb a tree, and would pull up to the curb to watch. They would gaze up into the tree to see what the dog was after, and after a pause ask me, "What's he got up there?" and I would say, "Somethin' small and mean." They seldom realized that the dog was just practicing.

This exercise was nothing compared to football games, however. I cut the lace on a football and taught Skip how to carry it in his mouth, and how to hold it so he could avoid fumbling when he was tackled. I taught him how to move on a quarterback's signals, to take a snap from center on the first hop, and to follow me down the field.

Fifteen or sixteen of us would organize a game of tackle in my front yard. Our side would go into the huddle, the dog included, and we would put our arms around each other's shoulders the way they did in real huddles at Ole Miss and Tennessee, and the dog would stand on his hind legs and, with me kneeling, drape a forepaw around *my* shoulder. Then I would say, "Skip, Pattern 39, off on three." We would break out of huddle, with the dog dropping into the tailback position as I had taught him. Bubba or Ralph would be the center, and I would station myself at quarterback and say, "Ready, set, one . . . two . . . *three!*" Then the center would snap the ball on a hop to the dog, who would get it by the lace and follow me downfield, dodging would-be tacklers with no effort at all, weaving behind his blockers, spinning loose when he was trapped, sometimes balancing just inside the sidelines until he made it into the end zone. Big Boy Wilkinson or Muttonhead Shepherd would slap him on the back and say, "Good run, boy," or, when we had an audience, "Did you see my block back there?" Sometimes he would get tackled, but he seldom lost his grip on the ball, and he would always get up from the pile of tacklers and head straight to the huddle. He was a perfect safetyman when the other side punted, and would get a grip on the second or third bounce and gallop the length of the field for a touchdown.

"Look at that ol' dog playin' football!" someone passing by would shout, and before the game was over we would have a big crowd watching from cars or sitting on the sidewalk. They would let go with great whoops of admiration: "That's *some* dog. Can he catch a pass?"

When I was going on twelve and started driving our old green DeSoto, I always took the dog on my trips around town. He rode with his nose extended far out the window, and if he caught the scent of one of the boys we knew, he would bark and point his way, and we would stop and give that person a free ride. Skip would shake hands with our mutual friend, and lick him on the face, and sit on the front seat between us listening to our conversation. Cruising toward a country crossroads, I would spot a group of old men standing around in front of the grocery store. I would get the dog to prop himself against the steering wheel, his black head peering out of the windshield, while I ducked out of sight under the dashboard. Slowing the car to ten or fifteen, I would guide the steering wheel with my hand while Skip, with his paws, kept it steady. As we drove by the grocery store, I would hear one of the men shout: *"Look at that ol' dog drivin' a car!"*

One day Skip and I were driving out in the hills. In a certain area near Highway 49 there is one tall hill after another for many miles. All these hills and the little valleys in between them are overgrown with a beautiful green creeping vine, right up to the highway itself. This vine grows in strange and wonderful shapes. Sometimes it grows onto the trees and telephone poles and makes ghostly forms. The green creeping vine protected the land and kept it from washing away during heavy rains, but when I was a boy I thought the whole world would someday be covered by it, that it would grow as fast as Jack's beanstalk, and that every person on earth would have to live forever knee-deep in its leaves.

Skip and I drove off the highway to a road right in the middle of that fantastic green vine. I stopped in a clearing to let him run. Everyone knew that the vines were crawling with snakes, so I was not surprised to see a monstrous copperhead slither out of the underbrush across the same clearing. I *was* surprised, however, to see Skip's reaction. He circled round and round the snake, barking and growling.

The snake did not like its privacy disturbed, and it snapped back at the dog, making ungodly hisses to match its foe's commotion. Skip got closer and closer to the snake. He would not listen to my shouts telling him to get away. All of a sudden, in one great leap, Skip came at the copperhead from the rear, caught it by the tail and began dragging it all over the field. Every time the snake tried to bite back, the dog would simply let go of its tail, and then move back in again to give the snake a couple of brisk shakes. While I was looking around for a rock to kill the copperhead, it headed out in a flash for the vines again, wishing no doubt it had never left home. For Skip it was all in a day's work. This nerve in the face of danger, which was Old Skip's strongest quality, would hold us all in good stead during the Episode of the Clark Mansion.

He was the best retriever we ever had. I would throw a stick as far as I could, then hide in the bushes or under the house. Skip would come tearing around with the stick in his mouth and, not finding me where I had been, drop the stick and look everywhere. He would jump onto the hood of the car and look inside, or sniff at the trees, or even go into the house to see if I was there. This game backfired one day. Bubba Barrier, Rivers Applewhite, and I threw a stick for Skip and then climbed up the elm tree in the backyard, hiding far up in the branches among the leaves. It took the dog half an hour to find us, but when he did he became extremely angry. He refused to let us out of that tree. We tried everything. Every time one of us came down he snapped at our legs with his long white teeth, and since no one was around to come to our rescue, we were trapped up there for over two hours until Skip dozed off. And we missed the biggest Cub Scout baseball game of the season.

His favorite food was bologna, and we worked out a plan with my pal Bozo, the clerk who worked behind the meat counter at Goodloe's Grocery Store down the street. I made a small leather pouch and attached it to Skip's collar. I would say, "Skip, now go on down to Bozo and get yourself a pound of bologna." Then I would put a quarter in the leather pouch, and Skip would take off for the store, bringing the package back in his mouth and Bozo's change in the pouch. Bozo enjoyed entertaining his friends with this ritual. They would be standing around, talking baseball or something, and when Bozo heard the dog scratching at the front door, he would open the door and tell his friends, "Here's ol' Skip, shoppin' for a pound of his favorite food," and with a great gesture would sell him the bologna.

One summer I entered Old Skip in the local dog contest, a highly important event sponsored by the United Daughters of the Confederacy. About five hundred people were in the audience, and I felt certain that Skip would win, since the prize was to be based on good looks and on the tricks the dogs could perform. About fifty dogs were entered in the contest, including Dusty Rhodes, Billy Rhodes' dog. Skip was the thirty-fifth dog on the program, and when he was announced and I led him out on the stage of the auditorium, everyone applauded loudly, because Skip was rather well known. Then a silence fell as I got Skip to walk around the stage two or three times so the judges could get a good look at the way he carried himself. Now it was time for the tricks.

"*Sit down!*" I commanded. But Skip did not sit down. Instead he jumped up and barked. "*Lie down and roll over!*" I said. This time he sat down and shook hands. "*Play dead!*" I shouted, but to this order he leapt off the stage, ran up the aisle, turned around and jumped on the stage again. The audience began to laugh, and I was by this time quite embarrassed. "*Sit down!*" I repeated. He rolled over twice and then stretched out on his back with all four feet sticking in the air. I had never seen that dog acting so ornery. I led him backstage and told him he had made a fool of me. I suspect now that Skip simply did not care about winning prizes, and this was his way of making fun of them. But when the prizes were announced, he tied for first place with Super-Doop, the Hendrix's Labrador. The judges said they were not impressed with Skip's discipline, but they gave him the prize because he was such a fine looking dog.

At night Skip would go to sleep curled up in the bend of my legs. When it was cold he would root around and scratch at me to get under the covers. First thing in the morning, after he had gone outside for a run, he would bound back into my bed and roust me out with his cold nose. If that didn't work he would make as much racket as a dog can make, and leap all over me from three feet away. Then he would walk halfway to school with me, turning back at the same spot every morning to go home. He and Dusty Rhodes spent a lot of time together during school hours, wandering all over town to pass the time and making general nuisances of themselves.

Later, when I first joined the Boy Scouts and began working on merit badges, I found out that not a single member of the Yazoo City troop had the Dog Care badge. I decided to become the first one, but I needed to have my knowledge of dogs approved by a veterinarian. I made an appointment with the town vet, Dr. Jones. I went to his office and he said, "Since I've never been asked to do this before, I'll just ask you some questions about your dog." He asked me about his age, weight, breed, and training habits, and then said:

"What about fleas?"

"What about 'em?" I replied.

"Does your dog have fleas?"

"He's got plenty, yessir."

"How do you rid him of fleas?"

"Well, I pick 'em off him one by one and throw 'em on top of the heater."

This must have discouraged the doctor. He started in on other questions.

"Do you feed your dog a good diet?"

"Yessir, I sure do."

"How many times a day do you feed him?"

"Oh, I guess about seven or eight."

"*Seven* or *eight?*" the doctor said. "Don't you know you're not supposed to feed a dog but once a day?" Then, shaking his head, he signed my certificate, making me the first scout in Yazoo County to get Dog Care.

5

We were close to growing plants, to the earth, and to nature's wilder moods. Many times I would go off by myself into the fields and woods that surrounded the town. I loved the little creeks and streams that trickled out of the hills into the delta, and most of all I loved the old Yazoo River, the river of the vanished Indians, which flowed slow as could be past the giant cypresses and elms and weeping willows, southward toward the Mississippi, the Indians' "Father of Waters." How many boys must have been claimed over the generations by the murky, swirling Yazoo? It was a River that was not to be tampered with, but we loved it nonetheless: the way it opened up and wound around, the decaying houses along its banks, the moss hanging over it from the cypress trees, the visions of the heroic Confederate ironclad *Arkansas* floating down from the shipyard near the sawmill to terrorize the whole Yankee armada at Vicksburg. Some days when I was basking lazily in the sun along its banks, two Negro friends of mine named

James Tuckloe and Robert E. Lee would come out from around the bend. We would throw rocks at the turtles, take turns shooting BBs at empty bottles, or climb high up into the trees and just watch the fishermen drift by.

In the Mississippi Delta there was nothing gentle about nature. It came at you violently, or in a rush; sometimes it was just plain lazy and at others crazy and wild. In the spring, when the muddy waters overflowed the Yazoo into town, and the shacks on stilts in the bottoms were covered over, we would see the open trucks with the convicts crowded in the back, their black-and-white stripes somber under the gray sky. Or a tornado would twist down and do strange tricks to the things it hit, carrying someone fifty yards and leaving him barely hurt, or driving straws into car tires like needles, or sending our garage across the alley into a field of weeds. On one afternoon a tornado hit while we were watching a movie in the Dixie Theater. We heard hailstones on the roof, hitting in steady torrents. A few minutes later, right on Main Street, I watched a huge rat, caught in the water where the gutter was, carried by the strong current closer and closer to the sewer that would transport him into the River, his mouth opening and closing in desperation as three little boys pummeled him with rocks and crushed open his head. Then one of them lifted him from the water, held him by his tail, and said, "You ain't goin' nowhere, Mr. Rat."

There was something in the very air of a small town in the Deep South, something spooked-up and romantic, which did funny things to the imagination of its bright and resourceful boys. It had something to do with long and heavy afternoons with nothing doing, with rich slow evenings when the crickets scratched their legs and the frogs made delta music, with plain boredom, perhaps with an inherited tradition of making plots or playing practical jokes. I believe this hidden influence has something to do also with the Southern sense of fantasy and the absurd. We had to work our imaginations out on *something*, and the less austere, the better.

When Bubba Barrier and I were ten years old, we found out where the Women's Society of Christian Service was holding its Wednesday afternoon meetings. One morning, following the cookbook, we baked two dozen oatmeal cookies, using every ingredient just as the book said, and then for good measure we added a mixture of castor oil, milk of magnesia, and dog-worming medicine. When the cookies were cool we put them in gift wrapping and pasted on a card which read, "To the Women's Society of Christian Service from the people of Yazoo City." Then we sneaked through the bushes to Sister Craig's house and placed the gift inside the screen door. Later we peered through the window as Sister Craig served the cookies and Coca-Colas. The first guest who bit into an oatmeal cookie chewed on it for a moment, her jaws working politely but with purpose, then spit with such energy that the crumbs landed at a point six feet away, spraying three other guests with the awful stuff.

Spit McGee and Billy Rhodes, who always had a special talent for finding dead animals, once broke into the home of Old Man Blane, the meanest man in the county, and left a dead dog, a dead possum, and a dead buzzard in the refrigerator. Once I gift wrapped a dead rat, labeled the package "perfume," and left it in the mailbox belonging to Old Man Blane. At other times I gift wrapped sheep droppings, six-month-old moonpies, live crawdads, grubworms, and hot bacon grease. When we were old enough to learn that in Mississippi, despite its being a dry state, you could order liquor and have it delivered anywhere at any hour of the day, we had a case of bourbon sent to the Tuesday meeting of the Baptist ladies, who believed all liquor came from the Devil himself, and watched from the bushes while Harry, the delivery boy, was attacked by the ladies when they saw what he was bringing them. "You . . . you . . . Get out of here!" one lady cried, and Harry swooped up the box and escaped in fast order.

Or I would pick a phone number at random from the telephone book, and dial it and say I was Bert Parks, calling from New York City on the "Break the Bank" program. Their number had been chosen out of all the telephones in the United States, and if they could answer three questions they would win $1000. "But I must warn you, Mrs. Wren, you are now *on the air*, and your voice is going into every home in America. Mrs. J. D. Wren, of Yazoo City, Mississippi, are you ready for *question number one?*"

"Yessir, an' I hope I can answer it."

"Question number one: *Who was the first President of the United States?*"

"Why, George Washington was."

"That's absolutely correct, Mrs. Wren," as Bubba, Muttonhead, and Henjie applauded in the background. "Now for question number two, and if you answer it correctly you get a chance to answer our big 'Break the Bank' question. *What is the capital of the United States?*"

"Washington, D.C., is."

"Very good!" (applause) "Now, Mrs. Wren, are you ready down there in Yazoo City for the big jackpot question?"

"Yessir!"

"Here it is: *How many miles in the world?*"

"How many miles in the *world?*"

"That's right."

"The whole thing?"

"All of it."

"Oh, Lord, I'll just have to guess. . . . One million!"

"One million? Mrs. Wren, I'm afraid you just missed. The correct answer should have been one million and three. I'm very sorry, and don't think I ain't."

People rarely believe that a boy we knew ran all the way around a very large block in thirty seconds, hence breaking every track record in the world. Well, there is some truth to this story, but sometimes one has to lie to tell the truth, and I had better describe this event in a little more detail.

There was a pair of twins who lived in the town; their names were Paul and Pinky Posey. They looked so completely alike that at times even their parents could not tell them apart. They both had long red hair, they were identically bowlegged, they had the same floppy ears and squeaky voices, and they wore the same clothes, which usually consisted of blue jeans and white T-shirts, minus shoes. They even got warts in the same places at the same time. Paul was slightly more intelligent than Pinky, but that was not saying too much. The only way we could tell them apart was that Pinky had four toes on his left foot, but seldom did anyone want to get close enough for a thorough examination.

In the summer of our eleventh year, a group of five or six boys from Greenwood, a town about fifty miles up the River, came to Yazoo for a two-week visit with their rich relatives. They were extremely obnoxious visitors, and since Greenwood was a somewhat larger town they lorded it over us, calling us country bumpkins and the like, and acting for all the world as if they were from Paris or London or Constantinople or the lost underwater island of Atlantis. I have met many snobs in my lifetime, but, to date, these boys from Greenwood, Mississippi, still rank as the biggest.

One summer afternoon Spit McGee, Bubba Barrier, Billy Rhodes, and I were playing marbles in front of the Yazoo high school, just minding our own business, when the visitors from Greenwood walked by and decided to show us how superior they were. "Here come them Yankees from Greenwood," Spit said. "Wonder what they're gonna tell us *now*?" They proceeded to tell us how wide the main street was in their town, and how big the houses were. "Why, the Yazoo River up there," one of them said, "is a lot cleaner than it is by the time it gets down here. Up there it's blue as can be. You can even see the gars wigglin' at the bottom. Down here it's all mud. You're gettin' all our dirt." They went on like this for a few minutes. Bubba and Spit and Billy Rhodes and I ignored them and concentrated on our marbles. Finally one of the Greenwood boys said, "And you see this big fellow right here? He can outrun anybody in this hick town." The object of this superlative was a tall hatchet-faced individual named Marsh. "That's true," Marsh said. "I can outrun anybody in town, and I can do it runnin' backwards!"

"Well, can you now?" Spit McGee suddenly exclaimed, jumping up from his game of marbles with such vengeance in his eye that I wondered what had gotten into him to break our icy silence in the face of the visitors' provocations. "Here's bettin' you five dollars and ten moonpies that we know somebody who can run around this here block in thirty seconds, and it'll take your man at least three minutes to do it by Bubba Barrier's daddy's stopwatch."

"Thirty seconds around *this* block?" the leader of the Greenwood gang laughed. "That's impossible. Let's just walk around this here block and see how big it is." So we all started from the front of the high school building, turned left on College Street, left on Calhoun, left again on Jackson, and a final left on Canal, arriving after a good eight or ten minutes' walk in front of the school again. It was not only a long block, it was the longest in town.

"Your man can't do it in thirty seconds," the Greenwood leader said. "Ol' Marsh can do it in three minutes, though, and your man can't do it in five."

"Meet us right here in front of the school this time tomorrow," Spit McGee said, "and bring your five dollars and enough extra spendin' money for the moonpies."

"We'll be here," the boy said, "and we'll make you look mighty silly."

After they had left, we all turned on Spit. "Are you crazy?" Billy Rhodes shouted.

"Shut up!" Spit exclaimed. "Just leave it up to me. It's three thirty now. Y'all meet me right here at three tomorrow afternoon. Bubba, be sure and bring your daddy's stopwatch."

At three the next day, after a night of considerable worry, Bubba and Billy Rhodes and I showed up in front of the high school. There, on the front steps, was Spit McGee, and with him were Paul and Pinky Posey.

Spit was at fever pitch, exhibiting a resourcefulness that was to rescue us from grave dangers in our big adventure later that year. "Bubba, you'll run the stopwatch. Paul, this here's the place you'll start runnin'. Pinky, you come with me. The rest of you don't do nuthin' 'til I get back. And remember, Paul, once you turn the corner out of sight, you stay hid behind Mr. Frady's house 'til we come for you." With that, he and Pinky Posey started walking down the sidewalk, in the opposite direction from the finish line for the race, and soon disappeared. Two or three minutes later Spit returned alone.

"Where's Pinky?" Billy Rhodes asked.

"He's hidin' in the shrubs in front of Miz Williams' house, just before he turns the corner for the home-stretch," Spit said mysteriously. It was just beginning to dawn on us what Spit was up to, but before we could question him as to particulars we caught sight of the Greenwood boys coming our way.

"You mean this is the little twerp that can outrun Marsh?" the leader laughed when he saw Paul Posey, floppy ears and all, sitting on the steps of the school.

"Why, I could whip him *crawlin'*," Marsh said.

"We'll see about that," Spit said. "You run first," he added, pointing to the incorrigible Marsh. "Pick somebody from your side to run the stopwatch with Bubba Barrier so you'll know we ain't cheatin'."

Marsh lined up at the starting point, and when Spit shouted *Go* he took off at a lightning pace. Soon he was out of sight and around the corner. We all sat nervously and waited. Billy Rhodes and I exchanged glances, while Paul Posey limbered up his bowlegs and did some exercises.

Finally, about two and a half minutes later, the Greenwood runner came into sight at the opposite end of the block. "There he is!" our antagonists yelled gleefully. "Man, can't he run?" Marsh approached the finish line, and as he did so Bubba posted his time at three minutes, six seconds.

"Okay, Paul," Spit said. "Line up." Paul Posey went to the line, and with the shout *Go* he started out, legs churning, and disappeared around the first turn.

"That little twerp's so bowlegged he won't even finish," Marsh said.

"His bowlegs pick up steam after the first turn," Spit replied.

Now the Greenwood slickers sat down to wait for Paul's appearance around the final turn in the opposite direction three or four minutes hence. To their horror, in a mere ten seconds, he appeared around that corner and headed toward the finish line.

"*Faster!*" Spit shouted. "*Speed it up!*" Billy Rhodes yelled. The improbable redhead, his features contorted and weary, his hair waving in the breeze, raced in our direction and crossed the finish line. I counted four toes on the left foot.

"Thirty seconds even," Bubba judged, and the boy from Greenwood who had been checking the stopwatch, by now wordless and in a state of shock, agreed. As we all patted our man on the back, the Greenwood boys stood off by themselves, shaking their heads and whispering in astonishment.

"That'll be five dollars, plus fifty cents for ten moonpies," Spit said, extending his hand. Our enemies counted out the money and then departed, too defeated to offer their congratulations. They never had the gall to face us again.

When they were out of sight, Spit said, "Let's go." Considerably more respectful of Spit McGee than we had ever been, we turned the corner where Paul Posey had originally disappeared and walked to the back of Mr. Frady's house. Paul Posey was sitting nonchalantly on the back steps of the house. "Come on, Paul," Spit said. "Let's go eat some moonpies." Spit kept three dollars for himself, and gave a dollar apiece to Paul and Pinky Posey.

6

When we were ten Bubba and I started borrowing his family's car. This was before he got his old red Model A Ford. Bubba had learned to drive when he was quite young; early at night we would sneak into the garage where they kept their grand old sedan and drive up hills and narrow dirt roads, down through the cemetery, anywhere that town adults were not likely to spot us. The country people loved the sight of two little boys driving a big Ford. They would shout and wave and come over to look at the dashboard, and we would sit on the steps of some ragtail grocery and eat candy bars while they examined that car right down to the whitewall tires. Then back down the hill we would go and sneak the car into the garage, and walk away as if nothing had happened at all, like Tom Sawyer and Huck Finn out on a nighttime lark.

Sometimes we would run across a group of Negro boys our age, walking in a group through the white section, and there would be bantering, half-affectionate exchanges: "Hey, Robert, what you doin' theah!" and we would tell them the names of the boys they didn't know, and they would do the same. We would mill around in a hopping, jumping mass, talking baseball or football, showing off for each other, and sounding for all the world, with our accentuated expressions and our way of saying them, like much the same race. Some days we organized football games in Lintonia Park, first black against white and then intermingled, strutting out of huddles with our limbs swinging and our heads shaking rhythmically.

On Friday afternoons in the fall, we would go to see the "Black Panthers" of Number Two play football. They played in the discarded uniforms of our high school, so that our school colors—red, black, and white—were the same, and they even played the same towns from up in the delta that our high school played. We sat on the sidelines next to their cheering section, and sometimes a couple of us would be asked to carry the first-down chains. The spectators would shout and jump up and down, and even run onto the field to slap one of the players on the back when he did something outstanding. When one of the home team got hurt, ten or twelve people would dash out from the sidelines to carry him to the bench; I suspected some injuries might not have been as painful as they looked.

The Panthers had a left-handed quarterback named Kinsey; he could throw a pass farther than any other high school passer I had ever seen. He walked by my house every morning on the way to school, and I would get in step with him, emulating his walk as we strolled down to Number Two and talked about last Friday's game or the next one coming up. We would often discuss plays or passing patterns, and we pondered how they could improve on their "flea-flicker" which had backfired so disastrously against Belzoni, leading to a tackle's making an easy interception and all but walking thirty yards for a touchdown. "Man, he coulda *crawled* for that touchdown," Kinsey bemoaned. Once I said, "You got to get another kicker," and Kinsey replied, "Lord, don't *I* know it," because in the previous game the Yazoo punter had kicked, from his own twenty-yard line, a high, cantankerous spiral that curved up and down, then landed right in the middle of his own end zone. But this was a freak, because not only were Kinsey and many of his teammates superb athletes, but they played with a casual flair and an exuberance that seemed missing in the white games.

Many years after this, sitting in the bleachers in Candlestick Park in San Francisco, I saw a batter for the New York Mets hit a home run over the center field fence; the ball hit a rung on the bleachers near a group of little boys, and then bounced back over the fence onto the outfield grass. Willie Mays trotted over and tossed the ball underhanded across the wire fence to the boys, who had been deprived of a free baseball, and that casual gesture was performed in such an aristocratic manner that it suddenly brought back to me all the flamboyant sights and sounds of those Friday afternoons watching Number Two games.

We also took to spending long hours in the cemetery. It was set on a beautiful wooded hill above the town. I loved to walk among the graves and look at the dates and words on the tombstones. I learned more about the town's past there—the people who had come to it many years before, the old forgotten tragedies—than I could ever have learned in school. My favorites were the graves of two great-nephews of John Hancock, the first signer of the Declaration of Independence; they had died of some strange disease many years before while passing through the town. They lay now in the sunshine, side by side and a long way from their home in Virginia. On a large plot of ground nearby was a sign saying that between seven and eight hundred unknown Confederate soldiers, killed in a battle not far away, were buried there. This, too, was favored terrain for me, because we were all beginning to read about Robert E. Lee and Jeb Stuart and Stonewall Jackson and Nathan Bedford Forrest, who had fought to preserve our Southern way of life. Sometimes we would bring our lunch, ham sandwiches and moonpies and Nehi Strawberry, eating in the shade of a big oak tree near the Hancock boys or sitting right on top of our Confederate dead. On other days we would come and play kick-the-can or hide-and-seek or capture-the-flag, until the lightning bugs came out and the crickets started making their chirping noises.

One afternoon, in the soft gloaming of a perfect spring day, we were playing hide-and-seek. Suddenly it became quite dark, with the beginnings of a dusty delta moon out on the horizon; I was "it," and I discovered I was completely alone. Big Boy, Mutton-head, Ralph Atkinson, Billy Rhodes, and Henjie had all deserted me as a trick, leaving me by myself in that cemetery at night. I restrained myself from running, and whistled "Anchors Aweigh" as I tip-toed silently among the graves toward the gate, past the tombstones of Peewee Baskin's, Bubba Barrier's, and Henjie Henick's grandfathers. I got out of there untouched, but I was so afraid I believe I actually felt a little pleasure in my fear.

We planned an elaborate plot that summer against a little boy named Jon Abner Reeves. We told him we would give him a quarter if he would walk alone, carrying a flashlight, at nine o'clock one night, half-way through the cemetery to the "witch's grave."

Jon Abner took the bet. Two of our friends promised to walk with him to the cemetery gates at nine and send him alone up the lonely road. At eight thirty Strawberry Alias and I went to the cemetery. It was a still, moonlit night in early June; the light of the sun was just going out on the horizon, giving the evening a ghostly orange glow before the coming of the dark. Strawberry hid himself ten yards from the witch's grave in a clump of bushes. He had a long stick, with a white pillowcase tied to the end; I had my silver trumpet, and I hid behind some trees on the opposite side. As we waited for our victim I spotted an old man walking up the road about fifty yards away, taking a shortcut up to Brickyard Hill. I signaled to Strawberry to be still, and took out my trumpet. I played a long, ghostly, moaning wail, as loud as the horn would go. The man perked his ears, gave a little hop-skip-and-jump, listened again, and then took off at a steady gait up into the woods, while we doubled over and all but rolled on the ground with laughter.

Soon we heard the faint sound of footsteps on the gravel, and there was Jon Abner, a frightened little boy walking among the trees, looking all around and flashing his light in every direction. When he got within a few steps of the witch's grave, Strawberry suddenly lifted the stick out from the bushes and waved the pillowcase. Then I blew a solemn high note on my trumpet, making the same terrible moan as before. When we looked out, all we could see was a faint wisp of dust on the road, and we heard the echo of small feet moving fast.

7

It was during the spring floods that year, when the whole lower end of town was knee-deep in the muddy waters of the Yazoo, that we decided to go in search of an old Civil War battlefield in the hills, where the Battle of Simpkins Hill had taken place. More than a thousand soldiers—most of them Yankees—were said to have been killed there in 1863. We had heard a great deal about this battle, but we had never seen the actual ground on which it had been fought. Our teacher had read us about it from an old book. It was called a "major skirmish." The creeks around the hill ran red with blood for days. Some people had tried to make a memorial park out of it many years ago, but they couldn't raise the money. But it had been a glorious victory.

So on this Saturday when there was a brief lull in the spring rains we decided to pack a picnic lunch and go have a look for ourselves. Rivers Applewhite, Billy Rhodes, and I met at Bubba Barrier's house, where Bubba was checking out the motor of his

Model A Ford in preparation for our outing. Just as we were about to drive away, who should walk down the sidewalk and say hello but our two Negro friends, Robert E. Lee and James Tuckloe.

"Where you goin'?" James Tuckloe asked.

"We're goin' up to try and find the Battle of Simpkins Hill," Billy Rhodes said.

"What's that?" Robert E. Lee asked.

"That's where a lot of Yankees got killed many years ago," Billy said. "That battle saved Yazoo from bein' beat."

"Yeah?" James Tuckloe said. He paused a few seconds and wrinkled up his brow. "I think I've heard about all that."

"Take us along to that battle," Robert said.

"Sure," Bubba said. "Hop in."

James and Robert got into the Model A, and we headed up into the hills in a fine holiday mood. The skies were quite gray and threatening, and from the top of Peak Teneriffe we gazed downward into the delta and saw nothing but water for miles and miles —all the way up to the cotton gin and the train depot.

"I'm sure glad the water never gets any farther than the railroad tracks," Rivers Applewhite said. Rivers had brought along a huge sack of fried chicken, which she passed around to everybody. "If it did get any farther, we'd be in trouble."

"My granddaddy says he remembers when the water got almost up to the hills," James said. "He says he remembers once nuthin' but water from here plum to Vicksburg."

"My daddy says one time he worked on the levee and kept the town from drownin'," Robert added.

Bubba's trusty old Model A chugged farther and farther into the hills. By now the land was reddish-brown and covered with immense trees which came right up to the road itself. A strong wind blew through the trees, and Bubba had trouble keeping the little car on an even course. Everybody laughed and ate chicken. Rivers Applewhite sang a song:

When it's dark-ness on the Del-ta,
That's the time my heart is light,
When it's dark-ness on the Del-ta,
Let me linger in the shel-ter of the night.

Billy, meanwhile, told a few tall stories and James and Robert kept up a steady conversation about various things they saw along the road.

And in that, lies a long and curious tale, so long that it would take another whole book to tell it. James and Robert's parents, grandparents, and great-grandparents had been in Yazoo for a long time. At first they had come as slaves and had worked the land, retrieving it from the swamps and the rivers. During the Civil War they were supposed to have been freed. The Yankees lost the Battle of Simpkins Hill but won the war, and one of the main reasons for that war was to free the slaves. James and Robert's people stayed on in Yazoo; now they made up about half of the town. But James and Robert went now to a separate school from ours, and their parents worked for the white people. I reckoned they should have been going to the same school with us because we saw them all the time anyway, and they talked like us and wondered about a lot of the same things. But at the moment we were eleven years old and heading into the hills in Bubba's Model A. None of us gave much thought to all this. That would take a while longer.

After another fifteen miles or so we came to a crossroads, and a small unpainted sign pointing to the left turn said *Simpkins Hill.* The hills and trees were overgrown with the dense green creeping vine which covered the entire countryside. We traveled on in this terrain for another few miles.

"I sure don't see no battlefield," Billy finally said.

"I don't neither," James said. "We oughta be seein' some guns right soon."

"I'll ask for some directions," Bubba said. "It should be around here somewhere."

Down the road we caught sight of an old woman shuffling along, using a stick for a cane. Bubba pulled up the Model A next to her. She looked at us out of old and bleary eyes.

"Say, ma'am," Robert asked. "Where's that battlefield on the Simpkins place?"

The old woman was silent for a moment. "What battlefield?" she asked.

"The battlefield from the Civil War," I said.

Again the old woman was quiet. Finally she looked straight at us and said, "Oh," drawing out the "Oh" as long as could be. "There's a whole bunch of graves and crosses and things way up yonder in them trees." She pointed up the hill. "Go way up to the top, take the first dirt road on the right, and it's about a mile in the woods, close to where Ol' Man Simpkins used to live. But that's *old.* Why you goin' up there for?"

"To see the guns," James said, as Bubba started up the Model A again.

At the top of the hill we turned right onto the narrow dirt road. The vines and trees now were thicker than ever, and we bumped along slowly for what must have been a mile. We crossed a shaky wooden bridge over a creek and all of a sudden came to the beginnings of a clearing in the woods, with a commanding view of a small valley tapering off below. We stopped the car and got out.

With Bubba and Rivers leading the way, we all tromped through the trees and vines into the large clearing. At first we saw nothing. Two red squirrels jumped along the branches of a tree, and there were deer tracks in the muddy ground. Then Robert shouted, "Look up there!"

Our eyes followed the direction of his pointing finger. There, on an immense rise away from the clearing, were dozens upon dozens of old graves, to the crest of the rise as far as we could see. Most of them were covered with weeds and the creeping vine, and some had fallen to crazy angles or were lying flat in the soft earth. Ever so slowly, we walked toward them. Thin strands of light fell through the trees, and Rivers slipped once or twice and got her blue jeans muddy. Some of the trees seemed as if they had been split in two by heavy objects and had grown back again, half dead and half alive; others had small holes in their bark. The tombstones themselves, mostly small crosses, were gray and discolored, or touched with thin layers of green moss, but on many of them we could make out some initials: *CSA* or *USA*. Under these initials would be: *Unidentified*. Farther up the rise was an empty plot of ground and a slightly larger stone which said:

"On this ground lie 150 unidentified Federal dead, killed during the Battle of Simpkins Hill, under command of Gen. U.S. Grant, Army of the Miss."

"Man, ain't that somethin'?" James said.

"I don't see no guns," Billy said. "I don't even see no trenches."

"Well, let's sit down and have our picnic," Rivers suggested. A huge log had fallen among the tombstones, and we sat on it and began eating more chicken, potted-meat sandwiches, and moonpies and sipping R.C.'s from Boy Scout canteens. The woods were deathly still. Far out in the distance we heard some dogs barking. I think we were all feeling a little sad.

"I wonder which way the Yankees came," Bubba said. "Maybe from that valley down there."

"Or they coulda come from them woods there and got ambushed," Robert said.

"My teacher says the Yankees got beat and turned and ran," Billy stated.

"Then how come so many of 'em been here ever since?" James asked.

"I bet they were all heroic," good old Rivers said. She put down her R.C. and walked among the crosses. Then she started picking some wildflowers and putting them on a few of the graves. Soon Billy Rhodes was helping her. He came to a tombstone that had broken off and was lying on the ground. "Here's a *CSA* one!" he shouted from the rise. "I'm gonna take it home for my museum." But he found it was too heavy to carry.

"Come on, Robert," James said. "Let's go explorin'." Robert and James wandered off into the woods, with Billy not far behind. Rivers kept picking wildflowers, while Bubba and I walked up the rise and looked out over the valley below.

"Boy, it sure is quiet here," Bubba said.

"Boy, I sure woulda liked to see this battle," I said. "Do you think—"

From the woods below came two excited shouts. Billy Rhodes and Robert E. Lee emerged holding between them a rotted old knapsack. "Look what Robert found back in there!" Billy said. We gathered around the knapsack. It had almost rotted in half, but written on it we could read another *CSA*. "I'm gonna take this home," Robert said.

"*Come here quick!* Come here!" It was James

shouting from the woods. We dashed off toward his voice, and about thirty yards into the underbrush we saw him standing solemnly and looking at the ground. We walked up behind him. Something about his look made us walk on our tiptoes.

"Look at *that*," James said. We gazed downward.

There, under an oak tree, was an outline of something sticking slightly out from the mud. It was part of a skeleton, with the bones of five fingers showing.

"Gosh," Billy said, and the six of us just stood there for long moments looking down at the hand. No one said a word. A breeze rustled the branches of the giant oak, and all we could hear was the rippling of the leaves and the dogs down the hill. I don't know how long we stood there like that, but it was a very long time.

Finally Rivers broke the silence. "I guess I'd better be gettin' on home," she said.

"Me too," James said. We all turned around and walked back through the woods and into the clearing where the tombstones were, toward the Model A in the road.

8

On the most vicious and turbulent bend of the Yazoo River, about fifteen miles from town out in the delta, stood a deserted plantation house which was called the Clark Mansion. Some said it was the nocturnal gathering place of the "river bandits," a notorious cadre of fiendish outlaws who roamed the Yazoo River from its source to its mouth, robbing the houses along the way or catching fishermen by surprise and making off with their money and their fish. Still others thought it was haunted, the spot where all the evil, invisible spirits and demons afoot in the whole of Yazoo County converged on misty winter nights to plot their deadly vengeance on mortal men. A small minority, including Big Boy Wilkinson and Henjie Henick, were convinced that the witch who had burned down the town lived now in the secret passages and underground tunnels that were said to surround the Mansion. Old Man Clark, before he died in the 1870s, had been not only a cotton planter but something of an eccentric architect and inventor as well—hence the secret passageways that were said to exist. It was even rumored that he had experimented with a laundry chute somewhere inside.

Whatever the truth in these things, no one in town had been known to set foot inside it in more than fifty years. (Spit McGee claimed that *he* had been inside it many times by himself, and that he knew the secret rooms and underground passageways very well, since he only lived four miles down the road and had to go *somewhere* to get away from his domineering old mother. Spit, however, was known to exaggerate the truth.) Strange moans and chilling cries emanated from it on cold, still midnights, and at least half a dozen strangers to the country, no doubt losing their way off the main gravel road two miles from the house, were rumored to have utterly vanished, never to be seen again on the Lord's good earth.

The Clark Mansion! Merely to write these words now, in a comfortable living room with a hearty fire in the fireplace and loved ones moving all around me, makes me shudder with the hideous memory of what my friends and I found there one night a quarter of a century ago.

I first saw it as a very small boy, when I was riding in the car with my father and mother on the main road. From that day the Clark Mansion etched itself in my memory. It was a huge, squarely built structure with a long, sloping roof; the sturdy branches of an oak tree, five hundred years old if it was a day, had pushed part of the roof upward, leaving an exposed area where mean-looking, stunted little birds circled in wild clusters. In the sunset of that long-ago late afternoon, a giant spider web on the porch reflected the last strands of light, and the cracked windows shimmered also with the ghostly orange. What once had been a porch, fronting the entire Mansion, sagged perilously and sloped toward the ground. The Mansion's gray, unpainted facade, the rotted weeds, the sagging nineteenth-century awnings on the windows, made the whole structure spectral, real only as one's darkest nightmares. The delta wind whistled through the exposed windows on the second floor, and what terrors must have lurked in the attic above? The red brick chimney stood gaunt and solitary near the south wall, partially collapsed also and covered with a seared gray creeping vine.

That house seemed to cast an unwholesome influence over the very countryside that surrounded it, for there were acres and acres, which normally would have been planted in cotton or soybeans or corn, of tall dull trees more dead than alive, their branches heavy with Spanish moss, and everywhere a dense undergrowth of thorny vines and grasses infested, no doubt, with rattlers and copperheads. A narrow dirt road wound its way two miles through this forbidden terrain to the house. The trees themselves were twisted into grotesque shapes, and none more so than the prodigious oak which had grown into the roof; from that distance the tree resembled a bloated and silent old owl. Behind the house and the tree, some fifty yards away, was the Yazoo River: a living presence with its murky currents and eddies and its fierce rhythmic roar. I first saw all this four years before the events I am about to describe.

It was a cold rainy autumn day; my friends and I were eleven years old. For weeks the people of Yazoo had been subjected to a growing number of daring, mysterious robberies, accompanied by two murders. Chewing Gum Fooshee was found hanged from the limb of a tree in his pecan orchard six miles from the Clark Mansion, and Old Man Ledbetter Ferguson was stabbed to death in his house on Peak Teneriffe. Mr. Ferguson's collection of rare old coins was discovered missing, and Chewing Gum Fooshee's money-box, which he apparently concealed under a plank on his front porch, was nowhere to be found. Bubba Barrier's mother's antebellum silver set was stolen, as was Billy Rhodes' father's prize collection of Civil War rifles and swords. One night the Delta National Bank was robbed of $65,000, and on the walls of the bank vault, scrawled in blood-red ink, were the words *Death to Anyone Who Looks for Us*. The sheriff, who had posted a $500 reward for information leading to the murderers and thieves, estimated that the following items had been stolen from various citizens of the town (not counting the $65,-000 from the bank vault): 65 diamond rings, 6 silver tea services, 39 silver carving knives, 9 rare paintings, $20,567 in cash, 7 diamond necklaces, 11 solid gold brooches, 11 record players and 34 radios (including my father's shortwave radio), plus countless valuable jewels and trinkets taken from the homes of the wealthier citizens, and quantities of food that would have fed Grant's foot soldiers at Old Cold Harbor.

Then an even more ominous note intruded. This new turn began harmlessly enough when the caretaker of the cemetery, Mr. Singletary, found a message written, again in red paint, on a large board and placed on the witch's grave. The message said, *"I have reeturnned."* This sent terror through the whole town until it was discovered that the message had been put there by Spit McGee; he was paddled three more times. Two weeks after that, and surely not by coincidence, the most beautiful tombstone in the cemetery, a twenty-foot cross with eight angels playing harps on top, which marked Mr. Cotton LeRoy's grave, had also been stolen, and along with it *Mr. Cotton LeRoy himself!* His grave had been dug open and the entire coffin had been spirited away. It was well known that Mr. LeRoy had been buried with his two valuable silver pistols; but how was one to explain that on subsequent nights Mr. Ed Bill Yoder, Miss Laura Byrne, Mr. and Mrs. Hart Hooker, the Reverend Cass Plimpton, Mrs. Luba Belle Harrington, Mr. Budwin Shrake, and Old Lady Goodie Mortimer were also missing, coffins and all? Nothing of value had been interred with these citizens, nor had they ever done harm to anyone.

The rumors spread and multiplied, and the town was in a state of complete panic. Nerves were at the breaking point. You will find it hard to believe just how jumpy everybody was. People locked their doors and windows at sundown. The sheriff came to our school assembly, telling us to beware of mysterious strangers and also of the enemy within. The preachers in all 29 churches prayed for an early end to our torment, and suggested that the Lord was repaying his parishioners for all their sins and omissions. Nor did the weather lift our spirits. Right after the Reverend Cass Plimpton disappeared, it rained solidly for seven days and nights, an alternation of heavy storms and quiet penetrating drizzles; the nights were foggy and interminable, swirling mists rising from the very ground itself; train whistles echoed down gray and empty lanes as they had never echoed before; and every dog in town bayed ceaselessly, almost prayerfully, to the nonexistent moon.

I will never forget the day. It was the afternoon of September 29, 1945. The rain had stopped for a few hours, but the skies were grim and threatening, and the first leaves were just beginning to fall, blowing in little gusts and circles on the sidewalks and the streets of Yazoo. Since it was not raining, we were able to put the top of Bubba Barrier's red Model A down. School was just out. It was 4 o'clock, and in the car as we cruised around town were: Bubba at the wheel, me, Old Skip, Billy Rhodes, Big Boy Wilkinson, Muttonhead Shepherd, Ralph Atkinson, and Henjie Henick. Naturally, since the beginning of the terror which had haunted Yazoo there had been only one topic of conversation. We had felt we owed it to our town, to its people, its churches, and its cemetery, to find the killers and thieves and grave robbers. Yet the more we discussed the dreadful crimes, the more befuddled we became. In accomplishing their deadly work, the fiends had left, for instance, not one shred of evidence: no fingerprints, no footprints, *nothing*. The sheriff had three men from the state university working in his newly established "science lab," analyzing mud, red paint, and diverse other items, but the lab was not very well equipped and none of the men were trained in crime detection. On the contrary, they were veterinarians. Still, there had to be *some* evidence.

The Model A was angling down Brickyard Hill, and took a sharp turn onto Canal Street, where we almost lost Henjie Henick. Barbara Nell Hollowell's grandmother, whom everyone called Mee-Maw, was standing on the corner and stared wide-eyed at the sight of seven boys and one dog dangling out of the rickety little convertible.

"Yes, Mee-Maw, it's a car," Big Boy Wilkinson said just as we passed her.

In front of the Gibbs' Florist Shop, Wash Gibbs was about to drive off in a pick-up truck filled with dirt. They were filling in the graves in the cemetery.

Henjie Henick broke the silence. "Something has to give before too long," he said.

"They say that criminals always return to the scene of the crime," Muttonhead Shepherd remarked.

"If that's the case," Ralph Atkinson said, "they'd be spendin' all their time returnin'."

"He's right," Big Boy Wilkinson said. "They'd be all over town right now."

Bubba ground the gears as we waited for the traffic light at Broadway and Main. In front of the Post Office Mr. Frank Patty, who ran the Delta National Bank, was talking in an agitated voice to Mr. Son King of the funeral home. Both had claimed that their products were unbreakable. Like everyone else in town they had aged ten years in the last six weeks.

We sat waiting for the light to change, everyone silent with his own thoughts. Rain clouds were gathering out beyond the bend in the River, and Skip began barking at the pigeons on the roof of Anderson's Drug Store. Billy Rhodes was sitting next to Skip, and he was looking toward the sky, at nothing in particular as far as I could make out. He was small for his age, and his crew cut made him look younger than the rest of us, but he was the fastest runner in school and he was afraid of no man. He adored Rivers Applewhite as much as the rest of us, and was always trying to whip bigger boys just to show off to her. I remember the precise moment

Billy spoke on that afternoon many years ago, because at just about the instant he did, thunder roared down the hills and Mr. Norman Mott dropped an Orange Crush bottle on the sidewalk in front of the Dixie Theater.

"*Wait a minute,*" Billy said. "*Wait just a minute.* If you were pullin' off these crimes, stealin' money and guns and coffins right and left, and you were doing it almost every night, you'd have to stay close by, wouldn't you?"

"It looks that way," Bubba agreed.

"And you'd have to be stayin' in a place that was completely secret and private, with nobody around, wouldn't you?"

Everyone agreed again.

"And you'd have to have plenty of space and elbowroom to store everything you got away with, wouldn't you?"

Again everyone assented.

"So," Billy said, emphasizing every word and speaking slow as could be, "what place would you pick near here that took care of all that?"

There was a silence now in the Model A. Then I heard myself whispering out loud:

"*The Clark Mansion!*"

Billy Rhodes had always been strong on hunches, but this was even better than a hunch. It made eminently good sense. Knowing something of Billy's involvement in difficult enterprises—his fights with boys twice his size, his feverish attempts to climb trees that had never before been climbed—I was not the least surprised, after I had supplied the inevitable answer to his question, to hear Billy say: "I think we ought to go out to the Mansion and have a look around."

Bubba's Model A was now at the end of Main Street, and he turned it around to head back in the direction we had come from. "You can speak for yourself," Muttonhead said. "You ain't gonna catch me out there in a million years."

"I wouldn't go out there with the whole U.S. Infantry," Big Boy said.

"Does everybody else feel that way?" Billy asked. I believe he was getting disgusted.

"*How many miles in the world?*" Henjie said. These words, to Henjie, were a good luck charm. He felt they would solve everything: all the suffering in the whole world, and all the hate and fear.

I wanted to say something brave, the way things were always said in the war movies; but I am afraid I agreed with Big Boy and Muttonhead, and so for that matter did Henjie, Ralph, and Bubba. I feel sure Old Skip would have been happy to accompany Billy on some wild excursion to that ill-fated house, but Skip was not Billy's dog. I also knew that Billy's dog, Dusty Rhodes, was even afraid of chipmunks, and had once been run out of a vacant lot by a pair of rabbits.

"*Chickens!*" Billy said, just as a few huge drops of rain began falling on the car. "I guess I'll have to take Dusty Rhodes and go out there by myself."

With this absurd pronouncement everyone laughed. Since the rain was coming down now quite heavily, and since we had all promised our parents to be home before the sun went down, Bubba dropped us one by one at our houses.

Next morning at the schoolhouse, our group gathered out by the Confederate Monument, where Spit McGee had promised to try to break his previous record of nineteen feet six inches for spitting Brown Mule chewing tobacco. Spit had surpassed eighteen feet four inches when Henjie Henick asked: "Where's Billy Rhodes?"

Indeed, Billy was not there. When the bell rang and we went to our classroom, he was not there either. He was often late in getting to school, since according to him his alarm clock did not run too well, but by eleven o'clock there was still no Billy. Many mornings he would walk to school with Rivers Applewhite, but Rivers was absent on this day also: doubly curious, because Rivers had not missed a day of class since she had the measles in the first grade. I was getting a little worried.

After school, when we sometimes went over to Spell's Grocery for a Nehi and a Hershey bar, I expressed my fears to Bubba and Big Boy. I decided to telephone his mother.

"Miz Rhodes," I said, "is Billy sick?"

"Sick?" his mother replied. "Billy hasn't been sick in three years. He's at school. He and Dusty spent the night at Bubba's place and they went on to the schoolhouse together."

"No ma'am," I said. "He ain't in school and he didn't spend the night at Bubba's. We let him off at your house at around six yesterday."

"No, it can't be," she said. "Is Bubba there? Let me speak to Bubba." Bubba assured Billy's mother that he was nowhere to be found. Then he hung up.

"Boys," Bubba said, "we've got to have a meeting. At Henjie's chicken shed in two hours."

We had had many secret meetings in Henjie's chicken shed, but this was without question the most important one we had ever convened. A large wooden box served as our official table; on top of it was the stub of a candle in a Coke bottle. The candlelight cast a flickering light on the walls of the shed, and the chinaberry tree outside the tiny window rustled in the wind. All six of us were grim and silent; only Old Skip seemed ready for action. His eyes were bright and he wagged his black-and-white tail furiously—in contrast to Muttonhead, who seemed on the verge of tears, and Henjie, who complained that he was missing Jack Armstrong on the radio. We all knew in our hearts where Billy had gone, and that right at that moment he was probably in the worst danger of his entire life.

"The question now is," Bubba said, "what are we gonna do?"

"Do?" Muttonhead asked. "Do nuthin', that's what. Let's go tell the sheriff."

"Yeah," Ralph Atkinson said. "We'd end up in jail. Remember the last time we saw the sheriff?" Six months ago Billy Rhodes had pulled the switch in a fire alarm box. The sheriff had caught us near the scene and told us if we ever caused him trouble again he would send us to Parchment, the state prison farm, to hoe cotton and eat fried boll weevils the rest of our natural lives.

"We've got to go get Billy," I finally said.

"We'll never be able to look ourselves in the mirror again if we don't go help ol' Billy," Big Boy added.

"Let's take a vote on the question," Bubba said. He banged the wooden box with a hammer and called for a vote. As such things often go, despite our terrible fears and trepidations, the vote was unanimous in favor of trying to retrieve Billy Rhodes. Even Muttonhead voted yes, although he added that he never looked at himself in the mirror anyway.

The prospect before us was not particularly encouraging. By now it was quite dark, and the rain was still falling in great torrents. In such weather, traveling on the muddy roads, it would take at least two hours in Bubba's Model A to even get near the Clark Mansion; what awaited us there was something that not a single boy in that group wished to dwell upon in any detail. Yet, there is something very strange in the actions of the human species. Even when we are the most afraid we can be lighthearted and giddy, and in such instances we sometimes move about as if in a dream, viewing our own behavior from afar, as other persons might view us.

For a while at least, this was the way we acted. We put up the top on Bubba's car and piled into it much as we would have done en route to a wienie roast or a football game. Big Boy Wilkinson started telling jokes, the same ones he had been telling for five years. Ralph sang our school song, "Yazoo, Yazoo," and Henjie, the only person I ever knew who could, belched seven times in a row. Skip merely whined in his growing excitement. I never knew a dog with such a longing for adventure.

Bubba had cranked up the car, and we headed down Grand Avenue to Canal and then Main. On this night Yazoo was like a ghost town, with all the houses tightly locked and boarded and only an occasional person to be seen in the streets. Even the street lights seemed dim and ineffectual. Fear seemed everywhere. As Bubba turned off Main onto the highway which would take us out into the delta, the bantering mood which had seized us suddenly ceased. All that flat gray land, the mists rising from the fields with their dead stalks of cotton, the impenetrable silence save for the rain on the roof, were working a most powerful spell.

"I wonder if they've done anything to Billy?" Muttonhead said after ten minutes or so.

In later years Muttonhead's question, which seemed simple at the time, would return to torment me. Who was *"they"*? Up until that moment none of us, not even Bubba, whose intelligence was always to be relied upon in times of crisis, had so much as paused to consider what we might be up against. We were not only unarmed (Bubba had not even brought his BB gun); we had no plan of action whatsoever. In our resolve to be noble and courageous, we were relying on luck and the timely intervention of the Good Lord. I suppose we could have done worse.

At last, some 45 minutes from town on the concrete highway, we came to the gravel road leading in the direction of the Clark Mansion. The road was treacherous with the mud and the bumps, and the Model A lurched and slid as it turned onto the final leg of our desperate journey. It was the blackest, darkest night I had ever seen, and I am certain that every boy in that car, which seemed suspended now on a bleak voyage without beginning or end, would have given the big toes off both feet to be back in the familiar surroundings of Henjie Henick's chicken shed.

"*How many miles in the world?*" Henjie exclaimed.

"Shut up!" Muttonhead said.

"The main thing to do," Bubba said, as he fought with the steering wheel to keep the car on an even keel, "is to be very quiet and to stick together. We'll park on the gravel road and head up the dirt road to the house on foot. Willie, you make sure Old Skip walks on his tiptoes and doesn't wander off into the underbrush. Willie and Old Skip and I will go first, and Muttonhead, you come along last and protect our rear."

"Who's gonna protect my rear?" Muttonhead asked.

For another half hour we lurched along on the wet gravel. Then, as we rounded a final bend in the road, the rain abruptly stopped, the overcast skies began to clear, and from the dark broken clouds a half-moon illuminated the whole terrain. There, from a distance of two miles, was the object of our journey: *the Clark Mansion*. Its outline, coupled with the oak tree which joined it like a dreadful Siamese twin, loomed large on the horizon, and even from that far we could hear the faint creaking of the awnings and the wind whistling through the upstairs windows. With one collective glance we took in the scene, and it was as one that we heard the surging roar, the agonized murmurous moan.

"What's that?" Ralph whispered.

"That's him," Muttonhead said. "That's the *Yazoo*."

As Bubba was bringing the car to a halt off the gravel, something from the house caught the corner of my eye, some brief flickering, some movement so subtle as to be unidentifiable at first. I looked again through the trees and the vaporous fog.

"*Look!*" I said. "Look at that!" Old Skip jumped two feet off my lap with these urgent words, and Muttonhead crouched under the seat.

84

"What?" Henjie asked, looking across the land-scape.

"I saw a candle!" I said. "Maybe more—three or four. There they are! See?"

Now there was no mistaking it, the slight yellow glow shimmering through the dirty windows. Some-one was in the Clark Mansion!

Silently we got out of the car and formed in double ranks as we approached the winding dirt road. I doubt if we could even have found it through the dense underbrush had it not been for the eerie autumn moon's glow. Taking great pains not to make any unnecessary noise, we tiptoed through the mud at an exceedingly slow pace. Muttonhead, protecting the rear, but lagging far behind, was stuck by a thorn and stifled a shout. Ralph stepped on a slimy moving creature, probably a water moccasin, but also retained his composure. Old Skip sniffed and panted but remained at my side. Henjie and Big Boy eyed the treacherous undergrowth for possible dangers, and Bubba and I whacked away at the branches and leaves with our hands to clear a tolerable path. We were engaged in this slogging, slipping, painful exercise for what seemed like hours. The hands of my wristwatch, glowing in the dark, pointed to ten o'clock, and as I looked at the dial Bubba suddenly halted in front of me. He reached into the mud and picked up an object I had not seen.

It was Billy Rhodes' red-and-black baseball cap.

"Tell Muttonhead to catch up with us," Bubba said. "We're not far now." Indeed, from a distance of about two hundred yards, we got our closest view so far of the house itself, and the glow on the panes was more pronounced than ever. "Muttonhead," Big Boy whispered. "Get on up here."

There was silence.

"*Muttonhead!*" Big Boy repeated. Again only silence. We retraced our steps fifty yards or so, and near a big cypress tree there were footprints in the mud leading off into the undergrowth.

"Where is he?" Henjie whispered. In the semidarkness Muttonhead was nowhere to be found!

At that very moment a roar came from the Clark Mansion that chilled us to our toes: an agonizing, bloodthirsty roar, followed by three or four others, one after the other, mightier than the sounds of the River itself.

"Come on!" Bubba said. "There's no time to waste. It's now or never."

We started running through the mud, sometimes falling down but getting up in a hurry, Old Skip taking the lead now, heading straight for the sagging front porch, Bubba and I following, as we entered what once had been a front yard and ran toward the rotting steps leading to the front door.

Have you ever had a nightmare in which a giant octopus, or an outsized black widow spider or lobster perhaps, suddenly confronts you face to face, and you are not sure whether to scream, or run, or just to stand still in your tracks? This was the feeling which seized all of us as the Clark Mansion loomed a mere stone's throw away now, immense as a monstrous aberration and old as death, and for a brief instant we paused, held back in the very motion of running, for here all of a sudden and almost against our will was a physical presence that had obsessed and beguiled and tormented us since we were children. Only Old Skip had not slowed down. He bounded onto the porch and began sniffing. Next Bubba, then I, then Ralph, Henjie, and Big Boy sneaked onto the porch, bending down very much like infantrymen under fire. We bunched up together, like minnows in a school, and crawled toward one of the windows, gradually lifting our heads to peer inside.

What we saw there was a scene that would remain fixed in our memories and our dreams from that day forward, as long as life pulsed inside us, as long as we mortal Yazoo boys carried the mandate of the Lord to live on this earth, and we would tell of it as long as people would wish to hear of it, and as toothless old men lying in bed all day we would describe it to our grandchildren and our great-grandchildren, and it would strike such terror in their hearts that they would repeat it and amplify it to their own progeny; so that moment of fear would live on and on, but exist never so vividly as in that exact instant that our senses allowed us not merely to look, but to endure the looking: because there, in the center of the big living room, were *seven giant Indians.*

9

Our eyes grew large as saucers as we pondered that incredible sight, for the Indians must have been at least eight and a half feet tall! By the light of the four or five candles we could see that they were tattooed from head to foot with ugly black tattoos of human sacrifices, of hovering buzzards, of scarecrows fluttering in the middle of tornadoes, of warfare, of murders—all these scenes of mutilation etched on parched, shriveled-up skin. Their beak-like, bloodthirsty faces made dancing shadows on the dirty, rotten walls of the Mansion, and they were chanting some gibberish at the tops of their voices, as if engaged in a solemn ritual well known to all of them.

We must have presented a most unforgettable picture, crouched there in the dark near the window with only the tops of our heads—from our eyes upward—showing above the sagging windowsill. We were transfixed by the sheer blasphemy of that ritual; we were staring so hard at those unlikely red giants that for a few moments we did not even allow ourselves to look around the room. But when we did, we saw things which fully equaled the horror of those gyrating monsters.

At first we only spotted a collection of harmless modern objects: a washing machine operated by batteries near the fireplace, my father's shortwave radio on the mantelpiece, several portable radios scattered here and there, a poster which said "Fly Delta to Dallas," and eight or nine beautiful paintings hanging crookedly on the walls. A black spider, big as a basketball, hung from a web over the rafters, and two skinny cats gnawed a bone near what once had been the stairway leading to the second floor.

But this was not all. Propped against the far wall was the most terrible sight I had ever seen: nine dirty, decaying coffins, all of them opened wide. Inside each was a skeleton, and the skeletons had been tarred and feathered! With their grotesque grins and their sightless stares, the skeletons seemed to have derived enjoyment from their base defilement. A belt attached to the middle of one of the skeletons held two silver pistols. Mr. Cotton LeRoy! Near him stood his tombstone, and on the stone the monsters had written, in red paint, several words in a strange language.

As our stricken gaze absorbed the varied spectacle which the Clark Mansion was offering on that historic night, we gradually began to notice that there was a direction to the giant Indians' chanting dance. At first we thought they might merely be letting off steam, or keeping in practice for their murderous raids; but then each of them picked up a long tattoo needle, which glowed white-hot from having been shoved into the fireplace. A large, dirty, overstuffed armchair, which we had previously not noticed, sat off to the side of the room with its back to us. Someone was in that armchair! I saw a small hand tied to each arm, and then the top of someone's head. And chained to a post near the chair was Billy Rhodes' dog, Dusty Rhodes.

"*My God!*" I said, nudging Bubba and Big Boy. "That must be Billy Rhodes!"

Just at that instant one of the Indians, who had been waving a tattoo needle menacingly in the air, must have heard a noise from the front porch. His homicidal eyes suddenly turned toward us, and he let loose a dreadful roar, pointing in our direction. His companions froze in their tracks and looked our way also.

Some kind of world's speed record was established in the next few moments. We bolted from our crouch at the window, raced down the porch, bounded onto the ground, and dashed around the side of the Clark Mansion. Old Skip had been leading us; suddenly he sniffed a brick. Bubba tripped over Skip, causing Skip's nose to press against the brick, and a small entranceway opened up into a secret passage. Following Skip, we scrambled inside just as the entrance closed behind us. The strange chamber we had discovered was cold and moist, and a winding stairway led upstairs. For several minutes we climbed the stairs, and finally we came to a spacious darkened room with a big branch protruding into it. Remembering the oak branch that lifted up the roof, we immediately recognized that we were in the attic. We wandered around the room, trying to collect our senses, and Skip sniffed at an old rusty laundry chute which dipped to the lower floors. All at once there was a desperate whine. Skip had fallen into the laundry chute! With a terrific crash he landed on the floor below us.

Bubba, Big Boy, Henjie, Ralph, and I caught sight of another set of tiny stairs leading to the second floor, and we sped down them to rescue Skip. But just as we reached the second floor, the wood under us began to crack and screech, the way ice slowly collapses on a frozen lake. Skip jumped into my arms. Henjie and Bubba balanced precariously, and Big Boy and Ralph tried to tiptoe back to the stairs. It was no use! With one final splintering, the floorboards gave way, and we found ourselves falling helplessly down, down, down . . .

We all hit the first floor in one great resounding thud, and as we looked up and around us we knew in our pounding, crying young hearts that we were doomed—doomed as no one had ever been doomed before. The seven giant Indians towered over us as we lay on the floor. Did I say they were eight and a half feet tall? At this moment, in our helpless condition, they seemed a hundred, their flashing eyes penetrated us to our corpuscles, and they merely stood there for a moment to relish the superiority they so clearly enjoyed. Henjie passed out from fright, and I would have done the same had it not been for a splinter in my tail, which kept me wide awake. The Indians walked across the room and picked up several wood axes. One thought flashed through my consciousness, and Bubba told me later that he was thinking exactly the same thing: was Billy Rhodes worth what we had gotten ourselves into?

The thought of Billy Rhodes, even in this moment of crisis and terror, prompted me to look over toward the armchair where I had seen someone tied down just a few minutes before. But the person tied in the chair was not Billy! It was *Rivers Applewhite!* What was Rivers doing here among these outsized fiends? And where was Billy? Rivers gazed out at the unlikely sight of five boys and a dog sprawled on the floor, and her eyes were wide with fear.

The Indians slowly advanced toward us, the axes in their hands. But the sight of his friend Rivers Applewhite must have sent Old Skip into a frenzy. He leapt from the floor, bared his teeth, and headed right for the Indians, causing them for a brief moment to retreat. Then one of them kicked poor Skip up against the wall, like a wisp of straw caught in a winter's wind.

Suddenly, from far across the room, we heard the sound of creaking wood. Then, thirty or forty yards away, near the staircase, a trapdoor opened from the floor. From the bowels of the Clark Mansion, who should emerge but *Spit McGee,* and then *Billy Rhodes* and finally *Muttonhead Shepherd!* Spit carried an antique gun, Billy had a tomahawk, and Muttonhead wielded a 34-inch Louisville Slugger baseball bat. The Indians gasped in their befuddlement, and as they headed toward the trapdoor Skip knocked one of them down with a flying tackle. Bubba, Big Boy, and I slowed down another by knocking over Mr. Cotton LeRoy, and Ralph threw a loose board at a third.

From the staircase, Spit McGee took quick but careful aim. There was the sound of seven shots, one after another in rapid succession, and each of the giant Indians moaned and fell to the floor, out cold.

A silence descended on the Clark Mansion. Spit stood on the staircase and surveyed the scene, smoke curling lazily from the barrel of his gun; Billy Rhodes and Muttonhead stayed rigidly in their tracks. It slowly dawned on all of us that for the moment, at least, the Indians were subdued.

First we untied Rivers Applewhite, who hugged every one of us and began to explain that the Indians had kidnapped her from her house early that morning, and that had we not arrived in the nick of time she would have been tattooed from head to toe.

"*Everybody shut up!*" Spit McGee shouted. "We

don't have a second to spare. I shot them ol' Injuns with my pellet gun, but I don't have no more pellets. I only had fourteen and I had to use double pellets on these big fellers. They'll only be out cold for three hours. We got to get the sheriff and his men out here in three hours before they come to again."

"Where's the nearest telephone?" Bubba asked Spit.

"It's four miles away, at Old Man Gollob's house."

"Willie," Bubba said, "you and Billy Rhodes are the fastest runners. Take out down the dirt road to the Model A and drive over to Old Man Gollob's house and phone the sheriff. Tell him to get out here fast! We'll try to tie 'em up or somethin' while you're gone."

Billy and I raced down the dirt road and got to the car. The skies had cleared and we made good time in getting to the Gollob farm. On the way Billy filled me in on what had happened. It was one of the most unlikely stories I had ever heard; somebody ought to make a movie of it.

Just as we had expected, Billy Rhodes had taken out late the night before on his bicycle with Dusty Rhodes. All day he had wandered alone around the grounds of the Mansion, finally working up his nerve, just as the sun was going down, to sneak up to a window and look inside. He saw the seven giant Indians and Rivers Applewhite, whom they were forcing to bake several lemon pies and to prepare some packaged Mexican food they had stolen from Goodloe Terrell's store.

"What could I do?" Billy asked, as I maneuvered Bubba's Model A at a frightening 20 miles per hour on the gravel. "I couldn't make myself leave Rivers with them Indians. So I just hid in the bushes for a long time tryin' to devise a plan. I got all wet and lost my baseball cap and was feelin' pretty low. And who should I bump into in the bushes but Spit Mc-Gee? He was muddy as a groundhog.

"I was so happy I almost hugged him, but Spit said, 'You dumb city slicker, comin' out here alone like this.' You see, Spit wasn't foolin' when he said he knew all the secret passages in the Mansion. He even used to *live* in the house by himself, until he found out the Indians had been livin' down in the tunnels for years and years. You know who them Indians are?"

"Who?" I asked.

"Why, they're the descendants of the giant Choctaws. They been livin' out here in secret ever since Old Man Clark died. They been plottin' revenge on the people of Yazoo who took over all their land. Well, ol' Spit found out all about 'em, and he decided tonight he was gonna knock 'em out with his pellet gun and collect the $500 reward all for himself, because he wants to buy one of them Buick convertibles and a Sears Roebuck fishin' kit, and—"

"But Muttonhead?" I said. "How did Muttonhead get together with you and Spit?"

"Well, the Indians caught Dusty Rhodes, who was

hidin' under a woodpile, and took poor Dusty in the house. I think they were gonna *eat* Dusty with their Mexican food. And about that time, it must've been around ten o'clock, we heard a lot of sloggin' and slippin' along the dirt road. Boy, you all sure were quiet! And we snuck out to the dirt road and ran into Muttonhead and took him with us. Spit and I figured you all was gonna make fools of yourselves runnin' into that house, and so the three of us might be able to catch the Choctaws by surprise. Spit led us down into a secret passage and we just waited there under that trapdoor 'til you caught the Indians' attention. The only thing Spit was worried about was his pellet gun. He was scared it wouldn't work. Say, you know what's down in one of them secret passages? A bunch of dead Yankee skeletons."

By this time we were at the Gollob farm, and we knocked on the door and got Old Man Gollob to let us use his telephone. I called the sheriff.

"Sheriff," I said, "we've solved the crime. We caught seven giant Choctaw Indians at the Clark Mansion with all the loot. Spit McGee's knocked 'em out with his pellet gun, but they're gonna come to again in a little over two hours. Get a posse out here quick."

"Who the hell is this?" the sheriff asked.

"It's Willie Morris," I said, "Ray Morris' boy. Get out here quick, sheriff."

"So what else is new?" the sheriff asked. "How

tall are them giant Indians?"

"Almost nine feet," I said. "With tattoos all over."

"They got good hook shots?" the sheriff asked. "They'd make good basketball players." He guffawed at his own suggestion.

"Sheriff," I said, "I'm dead serious. I saw Mr. Cotton LeRoy too. And we rescued Rivers Applewhite."

"*What?*" the sheriff said. Now *he* was dead serious. "Rivers out there? She's been missin' since this morning. Her parents are beside themselves."

"She's here," I said. "I promise."

"We'll be out there as fast as we can," he said. "Don't let 'em get away."

And sure enough, the sheriff came, and he brought about fifty men recruited from the town. They got to the Clark Mansion so fast, with their sirens on and everything, that they were there less than an hour after Billy and I had returned to the Mansion ourselves. They chained the giant Indians before they came to, and carried them away to the jailhouse. Then they searched all the tunnels and passages and found everything the Indians had stolen. It turned out from their confessions that the Indians were indeed plotting the slow destruction of the town, just to get their revenge.

"Boys," the sheriff said, "the whole town is gonna be proud of you. You've done a good job."

We caught one final glimpse of the Mansion that night as we headed again up the gravel road toward town in Bubba's Model A. It didn't look nearly as spooky as it always had.

Two weeks later the people of the Town gave a big celebration in our honor, the most spectacular in the history of Yazoo. All the church bells in town rang out for us, and they had a parade up Main Street with eight brass bands, Miss Mississippi, Miss Junior Chamber of Commerce, and the Maid of Cotton. Spit McGee was presented the $500 reward and another $500 collected by the merchants, and the townspeople awarded all of us many unusual gifts. Old Skip was given a fried steak a week for two years, a lifetime supply of flea powder, and $50 worth of bologna. Dusty Rhodes got a new silver collar and ten tennis balls. As for the rest of us, we were given the following: 25 old silver dollars apiece, a new motor for Bubba's Model A, seven free milk shakes a week for two years from Carr's Drug Store, free passes for one year to the Dixie Theater, a five-day trip to St. Louis to see the Cardinals play the Phillies, a beautiful blue sailboat, a three-day trip to Memphis to the Cotton Carnival, ten chicken dinners apiece in the best restaurant in Jackson, and a year's supply of baseballs. It was clearly our finest hour.

Yet six months to the very day after we captured the seven giant Indians, an unexpected thing happened. The culprits were awaiting trial in the jail, and one night they simply disappeared without a trace. Years later, when I had grown up and gone away to college, the sheriff's deputy, R. P. Dew, was laying a new floor in the cell which the Indians had occupied; he discovered an expertly built tunnel leading from under the jail to the vacant lot next door. What tools had they used to dig the route to their freedom? By what means had they concealed their handiwork on the night of their escape so that the sheriff and his men had been unable to find it? How had they managed to steal away from town without being noticed? These questions must go unanswered, for no one in the whole of Yazoo knows; it is one more mystery joining the legends of the witch's grave and old Casey Jones to bedevil the dreams of Yazoo boys of generations unborn.

All we know is that two years after the escape, the sheriff of Yazoo received a letter from the sheriff of Wahoo, Nebraska, describing a series of crimes in that faraway town so similar to the dreadful events which had happened in Yazoo as to make one's blood run hot with curiosity and fear. The sheriff wrote back to Wahoo, Nebraska, and said the pattern seemed more than mere coincidence. Having failed finally in Yazoo, had the fiends gone to Wahoo as the second best choice? Again we will never know, for the Wahoo crime wave abruptly ceased and has never been solved. One fact, however, cannot be disputed: the Indians have not returned to the environs of the Clark Mansion. To this day every afternoon at 4 p.m. a helicopter from the Mississippi National Guard descends on the grounds, and twenty soldiers armed to the teeth with bazookas, hand grenades, and machine guns search the house and the tunnels and secret passages for evidence of habitation. None at this writing has been found.

10

The news of our exploits at the Clark Mansion spread all through the delta. Our wild nocturnal ride in Bubba's Model A, Spit McGee's pellet gun, Billy Rhodes' red-and-black baseball cap in the mud, Muttonhead's disappearance from the dirt road, the trapdoor leading into the front room, Old Skip's unusual courage, Rivers Applewhite's close call with the tattoo needles—all these were expanded and embroidered and discussed for months after that memorable night. We were heroes for a whole year, and you can imagine the disappointment of Honest Ed Upton, Peewee Baskin, Strawberry Alias, and the others who happened not to partake of the adventure. But after that, as such things go (for fame is the least permanent of conditions), we more or less dropped from the public's attention, and we settled down to the less glamorous task of being boys in a Mississippi town again. This was much less dangerous than trying to solve murders and thefts, and although it was not nearly as satisfying, it was not without its smaller and more enduring pleasures.

For instance, every Saturday morning at ten o'clock in summer there was the "kiddie matinee" at the Dixie Theater; since we had a year's free passes to all the movies, we seldom missed a Saturday. On the screen would be the latest chapter of an adventure serial and a full-length western—Roy Rogers or Gene Autry or Lash LaRue or Don (Red) Barry. Most of the country people, including Pearl Hanna, would bring their lunches in paper sacks and stay all day, right until sunset, watching Roy or Gene or Lash or Red all over again, joining the town children in cheering the inevitable scene in which the hero dashes across the range on his horse at the speed of sound to rescue his friends from catastrophe.

The theater would always be crowded, noisy, and full of flying objects; one of the Coleman boys from Eden had his eye put out when someone threw a BB, and Spit McGee once set off a stink bomb that forced the owner to have the place evacuated. In the morning, first thing, there would be a talent hour, where we competed for prizes by singing a song or telling a story. Almost every Saturday Bubba Barrier, Honest Ed Upton, and I would sing as a trio "The Marines' Hymn," which we dedicated to all the Marines at San Diego, "The Caisson Song," for the Army in Sicily, or "Anchors Aweigh," for the sailors in the Pacific. Billy Rhodes and Henjie

Henick won prizes one Saturday for recounting the story of the Clark Mansion, but they both exaggerated their feats to such a degree—Billy insisting that *he* had shot the Indians with Spit's pellet gun, Henjie claiming that *he* had gone out there all alone rather than Billy, that we hissed and hooted them from the audience, causing a general reaction against them.

We also led the drive to collect coat hangers and tinfoil for the war effort, which would be used to make bullets for the soldiers to fight the Germans and the Japs, and we won prizes for these acts of patriotism. Yet we damaged our loyalties by selling chocolate bars and bubble gum on the black market, for these were next to impossible to buy in our time of temporary deprivation. That war was a glorious thing for all of us. The grand movements in North Africa or Italy were just for our benefit. Nor did it damage our reputation when the relatives of Mr. Cotton LeRoy spread the rumor that the giant Indians we had captured had also been German spies.

I kept a diary of the big battles, and whenever the Allies (the Americans, the English, the Russians, the Free French, the Chinese, and a few others) won one of them, I would tie tin cans to a string and drag them clattering down the empty streets. We never missed the latest war film; how we hated the Japs, those grinning creatures who pried off fingernails, sawed off eyelashes with razors, and bayoneted babies! The Germans we also hated, but slightly less so, because they looked more like us, and because the actor who played most of the German parts in the movies bore a close resemblance to our Methodist preacher. And the English (with whom we shared a language) and the French and Russians were good fellows, and the Chinese were curious but friendly, and the Italians (the accent on the first "I") were cowards but when captured were lovable and willing to change sides. Considering there was a war on, that town sometimes seemed mighty quiet.

Dominating this good old time was the image of Franklin D. Roosevelt, our President—his voice on the radio, his face with the dark rings under his eyes on the newsreels. He *was* the war to me. Because of him we worked in our "victory gardens," raising food on our own because it was scarce and you had to have special stamps to buy it. My father and I planted long rows of snap beans, potatoes, radishes, and a unique breed of swamp turnip called "zooboo," whose seeds Spit McGee had given us.

We looked into the skies for German and Jap planes, whose shapes we had memorized from 25-cent books on enemy aircraft. Because of the oil refinery a few miles from town, and the flow of commerce on the River, it was said that Yazoo had been chosen by the Germans as an important target, and when we noticed a blanket with a swastika, the Nazi emblem, hanging on the clothesline behind a house, we sent a letter to the sheriff warning of

German agents around the town dump. (The sheriff had just been reelected, and he naturally tended to believe us this time because our last alarm had been the Clark Mansion. Only later and with great disappointment did we learn that our "swastika" was an Indian symbol on an old Yazoo Indian blanket.) I promised myself that if Yazoo County were ever captured, I would retire to Brickyard Hill and the cemetery as a guerilla fighter, and if I were ever caught and put before a firing squad I would yell, *"Long Live America!"*

Bob Edwards had lived in the big white house next door. He had gone into the army when he was seventeen. Now he was fighting in Europe, and we exchanged Victory letters and I sent him oatmeal cookies (the good kind). One day a big package came to me from France, with a real German helmet, and the name of the soldier—Willy—carved inside it, and a German belt with its engraving: GOTT MIT UNS, and an iron cross, and German money, and postcards of German troops. Tolbert, the Negro man who did handiwork around our house and who would sometimes go with me as I rattled the tin cans down the street in celebration of some victory, was fascinated with that German helmet. Sometimes I would let him wear it home, and he would walk off down the alley doing a goosestep the way the Germans did, then turn and wave at me, snapping his heels and giving me the "Heil Hitler" sign.

I wore the helmet, the iron cross, and the belt down Main Street one Saturday afternoon. All the country boys standing on the corner came to look them over.

"GOTT MIT UNS," one of them said. "Now what's that supposed to say?"

"God with us," I replied.

"Yeah? Now ain't that somethin'? 'God with us.' You reckon they mean that?"

The day the Japs surrendered and the war was over, I was in the house with Tolbert, who was hanging wallpaper. We waited all day for the announcement the radio said was coming. Tolbert was unable to get much work done because of the excitement, so we threw the baseball in the yard for a while, and shelled pecans, and shot a few baskets, while the radio blared out at us from the bedroom window. Then Truman, the new President, came on and said the Japs had given up, and Tolbert and I shouted and danced around, and hugged each other, and Tolbert said, "That's the end of them ol' Japs. We whupped them Japs!" And we whacked each other on the back and shouted some more, and got out a whole carton of Double-Colas to celebrate.

11

Of course, the Episode of the Mansion and other events I have described were not the common, run-of-the-mill experiences for me. This is what I did on one typical Saturday in the fall:

Naturally I would want to sleep late, but since this was a Saturday during the school year, I woke up quite early to take full advantage of it. Old Skip got in bed with me for a while, and I just stayed there for a few minutes relishing that wonderful drowsy Saturday feeling. In my mind's eye I replayed the high school football game that Bubba and Muttonhead and I had gone to see the night before, when our heroes on the Yazoo High School Indians trounced Belzoni 34-0. Then, still basking in that Saturday glow, I looked out the window for the thousandth time at the line of pecan trees, and especially at my favorite, which I called "the witch's head" because of its unmistakable shape. My room was quite small, but nonetheless contained an unusual number of interesting items: colorful pennants from a dozen Southern colleges; the German helmet and belt hanging from nails in the wall; horns from a dead cow; a photograph of Bubba, Big Boy, Muttonhead, Billy Rhodes, Dusty Rhodes, Henjie, Ralph, Rivers Applewhite, Skip and me taken in front of the Confederate Monument after we became famous; a bookcase with books by Mark Twain, Zane Grey, Edgar Allan Poe, and Edgar Rice Burroughs; my father's old baseball glove; four chunks of petrified Mississippi mud; a football signed by Shortie McWilliams, star halfback at Mississippi State; a tomahawk taken from the Clark Mansion; a photograph of the 1944 St. Louis Cardinals; a framed collection of four-leaf clovers; a drawing of Gene Autry; and the rattles from the rattlesnake I killed.

At this point it was about nine o'clock. I got dressed in a pair of blue jeans, tennis shoes, a white T-shirt, and a green baseball cap with a Y on it, ate some raisin bran, and took Skip out for a run. In the backyard I absorbed all the smells of that autumn: the clean, crisp air, the wonderful delta earth. It was Indian summer, and everything—the earth and the trees, touched by the airy sunshine—was the lazy golden brown of that sad and lovely time; there was a faint presence of smoke everywhere, and the smell of leaves burning, and sounds and their echoes carried a long, long way. Wherever you looked there would be a truckload of raw cotton coming in for ginning; along the roads and even on the paved avenues of town you could see the dirty white cotton bolls that had fallen to the ground. Leaves of a dozen different colors drifted down out of the trees, and whirled and rustled along the lonesome sidewalks and streets. The weeds and Johnson grass in the gullies and ditches on the delta side were already beginning to turn brown and seared, yet so rich was the land that they still grew, half dead and half alive.

The county fair was on, and for the entire week we had taken in the many 4-H exhibits—the vegetables, and the bottled preserves in all the shades of the rainbow, and the pumpkins, and the great slabs of meat. A Yazoo girl had won the county beauty contest, and in a big brown tent off at the far end of the fairgrounds we had paid a dime to see Flora, the belle of Memphis town: "Watch her shimmy, watch her shake, like raspberry jelly on a birthday cake." Yesterday the air had been filled with band music from the football game at Number Two and the carnival tents at the fair; the high school band had marched down the streets, led by the majorettes twirling their batons, and way out in the distance you could pick up the strains of "On Wisconsin," or "On Dear Old Army Team," or "Dixie," or the sounds and singing of the school fight song, played to the tune of "Cheer, Cheer for Old Notre Dame."

Skip was tired out from his running, and now it was time to consult with Bubba. I went into the house and told the operator his number (it was 65; Henjie's was 27; mine was 243; my father's office was "1"). When Bubba got on the phone I wanted to know if everyone was coming to the football field, and he said everyone would be there at ten. I fiddled around with the radio awhile, and read the *Memphis Commercial Appeal* for the football scores, then headed up Grand Avenue toward the football stadium, stopping every so often to examine a dead frog or some other inanimate object or to say hello to some old lady.

When Skip and I got to the field we ran a few wind sprints and looked at the cleat marks that had been made in the ground the night before by our high school football heroes. Three thousand people had been in the grandstands and the bleachers just a few hours ago! I did a pantomine of a 43-yard scoring play, dodging the invisible tacklers on last night's exact route to glory. Then the boys showed up, including Billy Rhodes with his official Southeastern Conference football, and we chose up sides and played a rousing brand of tackle until the twelve o'clock whistle blew at the sawmill. The only injuries on this day were to Muttonhead's big toe, which he claimed he sprained when tripping on a cleat mark, and to Billy Rhodes' head, which he said Big Boy had mistaken for the football. The final score was 86-69, my team over Bubba's.

The afternoon held many possibilities, but this one began with fried chicken and biscuits at Bubba's house, and then a session listening to the Ole Miss football game on the radio. After that we got into the Model A, enjoying the hum of its new Dodge

110

motor, and headed toward town, picking up Kay King and Rivers Applewhite en route. Then we went to see the latest Boston Blackie movie. Since movies bored Skip, he curled up under a seat and went to sleep. Another spin around town, from the telegraph shack at the end of Main to the Country Club at the rim of the hills and the delta, and then on to Billy Rhodes' house to listen to the football results. We lounged outside on his porch and watched the leaves drift from the oak trees and listened lazily to the scores—first from little schools in the East like Colby and Amherst and Niagara and Gettysburg, or Allegheny and Susquehanna and King's Point and Lafayette; then the Ivy League scores, which were just exercises; on to the big Midwestern and Southern ones that really mattered, drifting slowly across the country like a great roll call of America. Then Skip and I took off for home, walking down the hills toward the quiet flat streets, hearing the echoes of all the dogs barking from many miles away, and making it just in time for hamburgers and french fries with my father and mother. After supper I turned on the lamp in my front yard and played football by myself, making up the whole game, racing 95 yards for touchdowns before 50,000 cheering fans, intercepting enemy passes in the dying seconds of the fourth quarter, kicking 46-yard field goals against 30-mile winds. Later I stretched out on the cool wet grass and, using the football for a pillow, just gazed up at the stars until it was time to go to bed.

111

A typical day in the summer was considerably more lonesome than in the fall, what with so many people out of town on vacation; but by nine o'clock I was out of bed and on the move. First I made some Kool Aid in a large glass pitcher, gathered some old comic books, and put a card table under a tree in the front yard. On the table I taped a sign which said, *"Funny books, 3 cents, Kool Aid, 2 cents a glass."* I might get two or three sales by noon, but rarely did commerce thrive in that stifling summer heat. To pass the time between sales I killed flies with a fly-swatter, pretending that the flies were Japanese fighter planes (one morning I bagged 23 in ten minutes near a watermelon rind), or turned over a flat stone and killed ants with a hammer, pretending they were German foot soldiers trying to establish a beachhead. After a while I just sat in the shade of the tree and watched the morning go by: the red water truck sprinkling the street, horse-drawn wagons going to town, a group of dogs all bunched together headed for the town dump. At noon it was time for a big glass of Kool Aid and a ham sandwich, and then to amble into town to see the latest war movie at the Dixie, walking along the sidewalks and avoiding all the cracks and finally taking a shortcut down the bayou to Main Street.

That day's movie was "The Fighting Seabees" with Dennis O'Keefe. After it was over, along about the middle of the afternoon, I was standing on Broadway and Main when I spotted a quarter at the bottom of a sewer. I went to the alley behind the Dixie and found a long stick, stuck the wad of gum I was chewing on the end, and headed back to the sewer where, after some maneuvering, I speared the quarter with the gum and brought it out. Then I walked down to the Bon-Ton Cafe and invested the quarter in a hot dog and a cherry Coke, sitting at the long counter and gossiping with some of the country people about the baseball standings or telling for the hundredth time our adventures in the Clark Mansion.

Next I went to my father's office and fiddled for a while with his typewriter, then on to the radio station to read the news coming into Yazoo from all the world's capitals on the teletype. There was a cotton auction taking place at Rap Crook's auction center, and I watched that for a few minutes before going to the Armenian's to watch him make bread, and to the Italian's to watch him make coffee, and to Gregory's Funeral Home to watch a funeral procession get started, and to the courthouse to watch part of a trial, and to the Catholic church to look into the windows and get scared, and to the bend in the River to watch the boats come past. Finally, on the way home, jumping over all the cracks in the sidewalk again, I stopped at Bubba's, who by now was back from weighing cotton at his father's plantation; we baked some more oatmeal cookies using our standard recipe of castor oil, milk of magnesia, and dog-worming medicine, then gift wrapped them and put them on Moosie Moorhead's front porch.

After supper that night I went out into my front yard for another private game of my own devising. Standing on my sidewalk about forty feet from the concrete steps leading into my house, I threw a golf ball, aiming for the bottom step. If the ball hit the bottom step it was a strike; if it hit the second step it was a ball; and if it hit the third or fourth steps I had to catch it on the fly before it got past a certain crack in the sidewalk. Otherwise it would be a single, double, triple, or home run depending just on how far it went. I threw one ball so hard it ended up in Ethel North's front yard across the street, and this naturally was a home run. Fortunately nobody was on base.

I had been throwing the ball for well over an hour. I was leading the New York Yankees 3-2 in the ninth inning and had yielded only four hits and one walk. Then tension mounted steadily, for I was going after my twentieth victory of the season against four losses, some 35,216 fans were watching from the stands, and the top of the Yankee order was coming to bat. I got the first batter on a strikeout, and the next one popped up, but then I walked two in a row. The count was one ball and two strikes on Joe Di-Maggio, when Billy Rhodes cruised down Grand Avenue on his bicycle and came to a screeching halt in my front yard. I got a fast third strike past DiMag just as Billy got off his bicycle, notching number twenty and finishing almost as strong as I had started. Furthermore, the old arm felt great.

"Whatcha doin', Willie?" Billy asked.

"I ain't doin' nuthin'," I said. "Just throwin' this old ball."

"I see you out here almost every night throwin' that old ball against the steps. Whatcha doin'?"

"Nuthin'," I said. "I ain't doin' nuthin', that's what."

12

Like Mark Twain and his comrades growing up a century before in another village many miles to the north and on the other side of the Mississippi, my friends and I had but one great ambition in the 1940s. Theirs in Hannibal, Mo., was to be steamboatmen, ours in Yazoo City, Miss., was to be major league baseball players. In the summers, we thought and talked of little else. We memorized batting averages, fielding averages, slugging averages; we knew the rosters of the Cardinals and Red Sox better than their own managers must have known them; and to hear the broadcasts from all the big-city ball parks with their memorable names—the Polo Grounds, Wrigley Field, Fenway Park, Yankee Stadium—was to set our imaginations churning for the glory and riches those faraway places would one day bring us.

Peewee Baskin went to St. Louis on his vacation to see the Cards, and when he returned with the autographs of Stan Musial, Red Schoendienst,

Country Slaughter, Marty Marion, Joe Garagiola, and a dozen others, we could hardly keep down our envy. I hated Peewee for a month, and secretly wished him dead, not only because he took on new airs but because I wanted those scraps of paper with their magic characters. That was before we got the free trip to St. Louis. I wished also that my own family were wealthy enough to take me to a big league town for two weeks, but to a bigger place even than St. Louis: Chicago, maybe, with not one but two teams, or best of all to New York, with three.

I had bought a baseball cap in Jackson, a real one from the Brooklyn Dodgers, and a Jackie Robinson Louisville Slugger, and one day when I could not even find any of the others for catch or for baseball talk, I sat on a curb on Grand Avenue with the most dreadful feelings of being caught forever by time—trapped there always in my scrawny and helpless condition. *I'm ready, I'm ready,* I kept thinking to myself, but that faraway future when I would wear a cap like that and be a hero for a grandstand full of people seemed so far away I knew it would never come. I must have been the most dejected looking boy you ever saw, sitting hunched up on the curb and dreaming of glory in the great mythical cities of the North.

That summer the local radio station started a baseball quiz program. A razor blade company offered free blades and the station chipped in a dollar, all of which went to the first listener to tele-

117

phone with the right answer to the day's baseball question. If there was no winner, the next day's pot would go up a dollar. At the end of the month they had to close down the program because I was winning all the money. It got so easy, in fact, that I stopped phoning in the answers some afternoons so that the pot could build up and make my winnings more spectacular. I netted about $25 and a ten-year supply of double-edged, smooth-contact razor blades before they gave up. One day, when the jackpot was a mere two dollars, the announcer tried to confuse me. "Babe Ruth," he said, "hit sixty home runs in 1927 to set the major league record. What man had the next highest total?" I telephoned and said, "George Herman Ruth. He hit fifty-nine in another season." My adversary, who had developed an acute dislike of me, said that was not the correct answer. He said it should have been Babe Ruth. This incident angered me, and I won for the next four days, just for the hell of it. And when the announcer set a policy that I couldn't win any more money I told the right answers to Rivers Applewhite, who thought I was the smartest baseball man who ever lived, and with whom I split the profits 50-50.

Almost every afternoon when the heat was not too bad my father and I would go out to the old baseball field behind the armory to hit flies. I would stand in center field, and he would station himself with a fungo bat at home plate, hitting me one high fly or Texas Leaguer or line drive after another, some-

118

times for an hour or more without stopping. I was light and speedy and could make the most unusual catches, turning completely around and forgetting the ball sometimes to head for the spot where it would descend, or tumbling head-on for a diving catch. The smell of that new-cut grass was the finest of all smells, and I could run forever and never get tired. It was a dreamy, suspended state, those late afternoons, thinking of nothing but out-field flies as the world drifted lazily by on Jackson Avenue. Then, after a while, my father would shout, "I'm whupped!" and we would quit for the day.

That summer, having never seen a baseball game higher than the Jackson Senators of Class B, my father finally agreed to take me to Memphis to see the Chicks, who were Double-A. It was the farthest I had ever been from home, and the largest city I had ever seen. I walked around feeling joyous, ad-miring the crowds and the big park high above the river, and best of all the grand old lobby of the Chisca Hotel.

Staying with us at the Chisca were the Nashville Vols, who were there for a big series with the Chicks. I stayed close to the lobby to get a glimpse of them. When I found out they spent all day, up to the very minute they left for the ball park, playing the pin-ball machine, I stayed there too. Their names were Charlie Gilbert, Smokey Burgess, Chuck Workman, and Bobo Hollomon, and one afternoon my father and I ran into them outside the hotel on the way to the game and gave them a ride in our taxi. I could have been fit for tying, especially when Smokey Burgess tousled my hair and asked me if I batted right or left; but when I listened to them as they grumbled about having to get out to the ball park so early, and complained about the season having two more months to go, and about how ramshackle their team bus was, I was too surprised even to tell my friends back home.

Because back home, even among the adults, baseball was everything; it was the link with the outside world. A place known around town simply as The Store, down near the train depot, was the main center of baseball activity. The Store had sawdust on the floor and long shreds of flypaper hanging from the ceiling. It sold oysters on the half shell, beer, and illegal whiskey which the bootleggers had gone to Louisiana to get. The baseball scores were chalked up on a blackboard hanging on a red and purple wall, and the conversations were carried on in fast, galloping shouts. There were two firehouses in town, and on hot afternoons the firemen at both stations sat outdoors in their shirtsleeves, with the baseball broadcast turned up on the radio as loud as it would go. On his day off work my father would get me to come with him, and we usually started with Firehouse No. 1 for the first few innings and then hit No. 2 before ending up at The Store to talk over the scores and the latest averages.

On Sunday afternoons we sometimes drove out of

town and along the hot dusty roads to baseball fields that were little more than parched red clearings, the outfield sloping out of the woods and ending in some gully full of yellowed paper, old socks, and roaches. One of the backwoods teams had a fastball pitcher named Eckert who didn't have any teeth, and a fifty-year-old left-handed catcher named Smith. Since there were no catcher's mitts for left-handers, Smith had to wear a mitt on his throwing hand. He would catch the ball and toss it lightly into the air and then whip his mitt off and catch the ball in his bare left hand before throwing it back. It was a wonderfully lazy way to spend those Sunday afternoons—my father and my friends and I sitting behind the chicken-wire backstop with a few farmers and their wives, and Spit McGee and his bearded father, watching the wrong-handed catcher go through his strange motions and listening at the same time to our portable radio, which brought us the day's action from Yankee Stadium. The sounds of the two games, our own and the one being broadcast from New York, merged and rolled across the bumpy outfield and the gully into the woods. It was a combination that seemed perfectly natural to everyone there.

13

Several times every summer I went the forty miles to Jackson, to the brick house on North Jefferson Street, to stay with my Grandmother Mamie, my Grandfather Percy, and my two crazy great-aunts. In Jackson I did not have to go to church unless I was foolish enough to ask to; I could remain a heathen there for weeks on end. There was a big magnolia tree in front of the house and several fig trees in back, and an old screen door with a hole in it leading into the kitchen. The Number 4 bus came by every fifteen minutes if I wanted to go to Capitol Street or Battlefield Park or Livingston Lake or the state museum. When my visits to Jackson were over, my relatives would take me to the Greyhound Station, and the loudspeaker would say, "Delta Local Coach now loading on platform 5, for Pocahontas, Flora, Bentonia, Little Yazoo, Yazoo City, Eden, Thornton, Sidon, Greenwood, Clarksdale, Tunica, and . . . *Memphis town!*" And the ride back home would sometimes be sad, because in the summertime nobody could put on the kind of show I got in Jackson.

Mamie, who had been the youngest of sixteen children kept a strange household going. She had been born in 1878, two years after the Yankee soldiers left Mississippi. She told me that when she was a baby, riding with her mother in a carriage near Raymond, Miss., whenever another carriage drew near, her mother would hide her in the back seat, such was her shame at having sixteen children. When the preacher came to have Sunday dinner with her family, Mamie always got the neck and the wings, because that was all that was left when the plate got down to her corner. But I knew that Mamie was so kind and gentle that she would have given away the last neck and wing in the world to the first person who asked.

Percy, my grandfather, worked in the place on Lynch Street that made potato chips. Every afternoon at four he would come home smelling of potatoes, and fetch from his satchel two big bags of chips, crisp and hot from the oven. Sometimes he would take me to work with him, and I would watch while he put on his greasy white apron, carried the great sacks of peeled potatoes to the machine that cut them into thin slices, and then transferred them to a big black oven. We munched on potato chips all day, from nine to four, and came home so full of salt and potato grease that we had to have five or six glasses of ice water apiece at supper.

In the garage behind the house, Percy built for

me a dozen replicas of steamboats, the names of them written in careful block letters, names like *The Robert E. Lee* and *The Delta Queen,* and he told me about the steamboat races he saw on the Mississippi when he was a boy. He let me shave him with his own razor when I felt like it, or scrape the dandruff out of his hair with a comb, and he would take me driving on the city bus all over town, two or three hours at a time, sometimes almost as far as Clinton to see the German prisoners working on the chicken farm. Nothing would get in his way when he and his "grandboy," as he called me, were out on the town.

To me Percy was old, older than anyone I had known, but he never let on that my pace was too much for him. He would do anything I wanted, from climbing the fig trees to marching along behind me while I beat a dime store drum. Two or three times a week we would take the bus out to the lake for a swim, and when Percy came out of the bathhouse in his trunks, the skinniest creature you ever saw, people on the beach would sit and stare and wonder what kept him in one piece. I would be a little ashamed of the sight he made, and go out into the water. Percy would follow me and dunk his head under the water to get the feel of it, and when he emerged again on the beach, walking out ever so slowly, he looked like some old sea-animal coming up for air, with seventy-five years of scars from rusty harpoons and fish hooks on him. Then we would lie in the sun while Percy rolled his cigarette and talk about steamboat races and his trips to Dallas when he was a boy, and then we'd catch the bus back home in time for a sack of potato chips before supper.

When Percy told me stories, he always came back to the one about the poor little boy who was not invited to the birthday party down the street, and watched through the picket fence while the rich children ate ten flavors of ice cream and a huge chocolate cake. That little boy never did get invited to those parties, and once even got his neck caught between the boards of the picket fence. One night I asked, "Percy, who was the little boy?" Percy said, "He was me, honey."

Mag and Sue, my grandmother's outrageous old-maid sisters, caused Percy's simple and happy life some trouble from time to time, although he was always gentle with them until they got on his nerves to the breaking point. Then he would say, "Oh, pshaw," and go back to the garage to work on a steamboat. Neither Mag nor Sue could see too well, and they had almost no sense of time, getting me confused with one of their brothers who died in 1905, sometimes thinking tomorrow would be 1865 or last week 1988. But they had great energy. Spit McGee, who once visited me there for two or three days, said they were more fun than hunting squirrels. They would walk around the house and the little yard all day long in their flowing black dresses, running into doors and trees, knocking things off tables. At times they would bump into each other and say, "Excuse me," then push off again in opposite directions. One day I saw Mag trying to strike up a conversation with the garbage can, and another time Sue was talking very seriously to a broomstick.

At night, as Percy and I lay half awake, I would hear their voices—Mamie's, Mag's, Sue's—from the parlor. I loved to lie in the next room, in that lulled awareness just before sleep, and hear the ticktock of the old clock and the quiet, aimless talk: about "Momma" and "Poppa," my great-grandparents, or the other brothers long since dead, or the brother who went to New York at the turn of the century and was never heard from again.

My two great-aunts were ideal victims. When I was eight, I sent for a gadget described as an "ultra-mike" in a toy catalogue. It cost two dollars, and must have been the best investment I ever made. It looked like a cheap version of a regular radio microphone, the kind that real radio announcers talk into; all you had to do to break into a radio broadcast was to clamp a hook on a wire to any kind of electric outlet—a lamp would do, or a fan, or a refrigerator. Then you would talk into the ultra-mike, and your voice would come out of the radio as if it were the usual program.

I would hook up the ultra-mike in the back room while Mag and Sue sat listening to the radio in the parlor. Then I would say, "We interrupt this program to bring you a special announcement. *The Yankees are coming! They are ten minutes away! I repeat: The Yankee soldiers are on their way!*" Then Mag and Sue, holding their dresses above their knees to run better, would leap out of their chairs and dash to my grandmother: "Marion, Marion, did you hear? They're comin'! They're on their way!"

"*Who* is comin'?" my grandmother would reply. And they would repeat, "The Yankee soldiers, that's what the radio said."

"Oh, that's just the boy," my grandmother would say, "foolin' you again. That was a long time ago anyway."

"Oh, that boy!" my aunts would shout, and go sit down again. But they were such good material that in two or three hours I could try the same thing all over again, and more often than not it worked.

Sometimes in the summer I wouldn't even let them know I was coming. I would catch the Greyhound in Yazoo and ride over to Jackson by myself, then hop the Number 4 bus and head out to Jefferson Street. From the bus stop I would detour through the neighbors' backyard and sneak quietly in through the back door of the little house, hiding myself in a hall closet near the parlor.

Mamie, Percy, Mag, and Sue were sitting in the big overstuffed chairs in the parlor. By now it was about 10 o'clock in the morning, and they were all fanning themselves with the paper fans distributed by the Wright & Ferguson Funeral Home. They were just sitting there, fanning themselves and not saying much, the only noise being the clatter and bustle from the Jitney Jungle across the street.

"Oh, ain't it a *scorcher*?" I heard Mag say.

"Oh, *ain't* it a scorcher?" Sue repeated.

"Ten o'clock in the mornin' and already it's unbearable," Mag said.

"Just *unbearable*," Sue said.

Then silence again. From the closet I could see that Percy was drinking a lemonade and gazing out the window. Mamie, having finished her housework at about 8 a.m., was resting in her chair.

On all such occasions I brought along a pocketful of pennies, and now I set about my task. Quiet as could be I opened the door of the closet and tossed a penny into the parlor. It bounced on the mahogany table and then fell onto the floor.

The four of them cocked their heads at the sound of the penny. Nothing was said for a few seconds.

"What was that noise?" Mag finally asked.

"I thought I heard somethin', too," Sue said.

"Came from over there," Mag said.

Then they let the subject drop, and lapsed again into silence.

I took another penny and threw it in the direction of the fireplace. It struck the mantlepiece and fell into a wastebasket.

"What was *that*?" This time Percy asked the question.

128

"Something fell off the mantle," Mamie said. She got up and looked around but couldn't find the penny. Mag and Sue got up and circled the room twice, looking for nothing in particular that I could see, then sat down.

I opened the closet door a third time and tossed a penny up against the bookcase. It knocked a *Saturday Evening Post* off the shelf.

Now all four of them rose at the same time. Sue went over to the bookcase and looked quizzically at the *Saturday Evening Post* on the floor. She picked it up and put it back, not noticing the penny.

I waited five minutes this time.

"It's a *scorcher*!" Mag said.

"I felt a breeze a little while ago," Mamie said. "It sure felt good."

"There's another breeze!" Sue said.

"It ain't much of one, though," Mag added.

Plunk. The penny hit the brass spittoon next to Percy's chair and landed inside. Percy bolted in his chair. Mag and Sue stood up and stared.

"I heard somethin' else," Mag said, as Percy looked down at the spittoon.

Ding. The penny hit the top of the clock this time, bounced off and fell to the floor. Mamie reached down and picked up the penny.

"Why, it's a penny," she said.

"Where did it come from?" Mag wondered.

"Is that boy here?" Percy suddenly asked.

"Why, no," Mamie said. "He ain't supposed to come 'til next week."

"That boy's *here*," Percy said. He got up and searched under the sofa, then headed for the hall and looked behind the furnace. He opened the door of the closet, and there I was.

"It's him all right!" Percy said, pulling me by the arm out of the closet. "I knew it all along."

"The boy's here!" Mag exclaimed, and there was a great whirl of activity as I came into the parlor with Percy: embracing and laughing and shouting. Then Mamie brought out a cold lemon pie and said, "I never saw a boy who could do such tricks with pennies."

We would take long walks, the five of us, down shaded streets, past the mansion of the man they told me had stolen all the money from "the state" in the 1920s and escaped to Chicago, and on to the State Capitol surrounded by the beautiful magnolia trees, to look for envelopes with foreign stamps on them in the big garbage bin where they threw things away. We would go inside the Capitol and browse around in the Confederate museum, looking at those countless battle flags and banners, dull and shriveled with age, or the Indian mummy all dressed up in her coffin, or the statue of the dwarflike Senator Bilbo, who always made me laugh. Then we would make the slow walk back home in the dusk past the people sitting on their porches rocking slowly, almost sadly, and talk about what we would do tomorrow.

Best of all, as always, were the baseball games, the ultimate joy of those childhood summers. The

Senators were in the Southeastern League, and they played in the state fairgrounds against teams from Meridian, Vicksburg, Pensacola, Montgomery, Selma, Anniston, and Gadsden. I remember the names of my heroes of the 1940s—Duke Doolittle, Tommy Davis, Bill Adair, Banks McDowell, Vern Bickford, Leo Grose, Lew Flick, Dave Caliento, and many another who stuck there, not quite able to make it past Class B. Class B, however, was good enough for me. I read avidly about those men in the papers, sometimes taking notes on them. I sent them fan mail and donated quarters to the special "nights" they had for them. Only Percy appreciated all this; for the others the game might just as well have been ice hockey, or water polo. One night when Percy was sick (he had fallen off the roof of the house while cleaning the leaves out of the gutters and had bitten his tongue), I took Mamie and Mag down to the fairgrounds to see a game. Both of them went to sleep. Mag woke up in the eighth inning and asked what the score was. "It's nuthin' to nuthin'," I said. "Nuthin' to nuthin'?" she replied. "Why, ain't neither one of 'em any good!"

It was torture, waiting out the long summer day until five thirty when Percy and I could set out on the long walk to the fairgrounds. Several times I got down on my knees and prayed, during bad weather, that the game would not be rained out. We would get to the gate just when it opened, in time to watch both teams taking batting practice and infield.

And the smells of that baseball park! The peanuts and the sizzling "Pronto Pups," the fresh green grass in the outfield, the resin. And the echoing crack when the bat hit the ball, the lazy outfielders casually drifting under a tall fly or waving goodbye when a ball went over the fence. When the game got close, Percy and I would hold hands in our fear that something might go wrong. And when Tommy Davis hit a home run to break up a game, Percy and I would embrace each other in joy, and hurry home to talk about it with Mamie, who would be waiting with a midnight snack of shrimp and fried chicken and cold milk and potato chips. "When Tommy hit that home run," Percy would say, "they wanted to tear the grandstand down and give it to him right there." "Sure 'nuff?" Mamie asked. "Was it a curve or a fast one?" for we had coached her to ask such questions. Lying sleepily in bed that night, Percy and I would talk about the game. "I'll sleep good tonight after what Tommy did," Percy would say. The next morning I would write Tommy Davis and tell him that surely was the best home run ever hit.

How I hated the end of summer to come! Early June was the perfect time, because the whole summer stretched out before me luxuriously; but as the days passed I would count them off with horror, for the day would surely come when the summer was all over forever, and there would be new shoes that were always too small, and scratchy new clothes, and blank new looseleaf notebooks, and monotonous classroom hours under the scrutiny of Miss Abbott or one of her colleagues. In my bed in Jackson one early morning in late August, I stretched drowsily on the sheets and smelled the cool, crisp day and that coolness brought with it a feeling of the softest, most bittersweet sadness. *Summer's almost gone,* I whispered to myself, remembering how limitless it had seemed back in June. And I promised myself, lying in that familiar old bed, to get as much out of the remaining precious days as time would allow.

The day my aunt Sue died, they took me out of school, and we drove to Jackson for the funeral. Afterwards Percy took me by the hand to Woolworth's, to buy me whatever I wanted. He told me, "Now don't you be sad." That day I remember I promised myself that if *Percy* ever died, I would shoot myself with the pistol my father kept under the mattress at home. But I knew that Percy would never die.

14

One autumn afternoon not too long after the Clark Mansion rescue, my father and I had Skip out hunting squirrels in the woods at the delta end of the county, near Spit McGee's house. There was a slight rustling in the underbrush. The dog suddenly froze, then took a neat bounding leap, crashing in after the sound. Almost as suddenly he came out, the most woebegone dog in the world. A skunk strutted out into the opening and down the trail. The dog had the foul yellow stuff all over him, and smelled so awful we had to put handkerchiefs to our noses; even his eyes looked sick. We walked back to the clearing and wrapped him in a blanket, and took him home and bathed him, not once but twice, in tomato juice. We did not want to lay our sights on him again for days, and until the smell wore off he was the most unenthusiastic creature I ever saw.

At first we had trained our big dogs, and then the fox terriers, to go into the woods. Skip was the best of all, for he walked the woods with a natural sense of the impossible. The delta woods, when I was a boy, were a living thing for me. There were stretches, in the dank swamp bottoms, that stayed almost wholly dark, even on the brightest of days. The tall, thick trees were covered with vines and creeping plants, and on a gray December afternoon the silence was so cold and complete that as a small boy I became frightened, and stayed close to my father.

He taught me how to note landmarks so we would not get lost as we went deeper into the woods: a hickory had a gnarled limb like a broken arm, or an ash was split in two, probably by lightning. Sometimes he would make his own marks, with paper or empty shotgun shells, and he always kept a close eye on the compass. Three or four times men had gotten hopelessly lost in these hidden places, and someone had to organize search parties, or get the sheriff and his deputies to circle around and around in the woods in search of footprints or empty shells or signs of fires.

As we walked along the thin trail, fighting the mosquitoes that swarmed at us despite the ointment on our skin, the sun would suddenly open up some half-clearing, and giant spider webs would shimmer and toss in the light. My father would stand dead in his tracks, motioning to me to be still, and he would point to a deer farther down the path, looking at us a brief moment before scampering away into the trees. We never hunted deer; my father was against it. We came to these woods chiefly to shoot the wild squirrels, gray and red and sometimes black; and the squirrel dumplings my mother made, even if we had to spit out the buckshot while eating them, were always worth the hardest day's walk. We had big squirrel cookouts in our back yard and invited all my friends, and one night Big Boy Wilkinson ate four fried squirrels by himself and drank ten Double-Colas.

On other days we would rise before dawn and drive out the flat roads past the dead cotton stalks in the fields, making it to the woods just as the sun was beginning to show. Then we would hear the chatter and rustling of all the birds and beasts, and the dog would be ready to tear a muscle to get into the woods and see what was there. In the bottoms, the ground was so sloggy that our boots would make faint oozing sounds, and our footmarks would slowly fill up with water as we walked. And there were days when the air was so thick with mosquitoes in that raw wilderness that we had to give up, and either try to find someplace else or go home.

These woods were so much a part of our life, only a thirty- or forty-minute drive from the town, that I grew up taking them for granted. Only later did I realize that they were the last and largest of the delta forest, that it was only at the bottom of that $\triangle$ of the delta, where we were, that the remnants of the old unbroken wilderness had been left intact. On the way home, very late, you could watch out the front window of the car as the bugs splattered softly on its windshield, tattooing the glass with delta things.

My father and I were in a stretch of these woods on December 7, 1941, when I was seven; I can remember the day by the news about Pearl Harbor that greeted us when we went home. And we had been there many times before then. At first I used a .22 rifle, though my father once let me shoot his .12 gauge shotgun—out of nothing but mischief, because after I squeezed the trigger that gun knocked me for a twisting nosedive into the mud. One afternoon, when I was nine, we were walking through the woods with one of the town firemen. All of a sudden he shouted "Jump!" just as my foot hit something soft and wet, and I leaped as high as I could go. "Look at *that*," the fireman said, rolling out the "that," and my father went "*wheew*." There was a rattlesnake that looked eight feet long, right in my path. "Let the boy shoot him," the fireman said, and I aimed my .22 and killed him through the head. The fireman pulled out his knife and cut off his rattles and handed them to me. The next day I took the rattles to school, and all the country boys gathered around and Spit McGee said, "He was a *big* 'un." But Miss Abbott, the teacher, found out about it and made me take my trophy home. If the dust from the insides got in my eyes, she said, I would be blinded for life. My father said Miss Abbott was quoting an old wives' tale, and Spit said rattler dust would actually make you see better than before.

On my twelfth birthday I got a shiny new .16 gauge smelling richly of oil, and the next time we went into the woods I wasted a whole box of shells shooting at nothing and the dogs thought I had gone insane.

Several times, in the woods around Panther Creek, we ran across a man my father knew—a hanger-on, he called him. The man lived right in the middle of the woods, in a little wood shanty he had made for himself. He had a scraggly black beard and wore beat-up khakis and a slouch hat; in the back of his shack was a small vegetable garden. The game wardens ignored him, and he lived off the animals he could kill and made a little money now and then guiding the deer hunters through the woods. My father always asked him how the hunting was going, and later he told me the man would eat anything just so it wasn't alive—and even then he might eat it if the gravy was good.

We did cane-pole fishing, both to save money and because it was lazier; for we seldom worked very hard on these trips to Wolf or Five-Mile Lakes. The most work came the night before, when we hired a couple of Negro children at a quarter each and went back to the town dump, where all the garbage in town was piled, to catch roaches for bait. We had a big wire basket with a lid on top, and we sighted the roaches by flashlight, trapping them in our hands and dropping them into the basket. Early the next morning we would drive out into the same delta country, only not as far, rent a boat from a sharecropper, and spend the day drifting around the water. When the biting was good we might bring home twenty or thirty white perch or bream or goggle-eyes; when it was bad we would go to sleep in the boat. We would stop at some crossroads store on the way back to stretch and have a cold drink and talk about the fishing with the men who sat out front whittling and chewing tobacco, spitting between the cracks of the porch floor and talking all the while. When we got home we would clean the fish on the back steps and eat them fried, with a crust as delicious as the fish itself. I would hate to say how many of these fish Big Boy Wilkinson could eat.

I remember one of these afternoons—one of the last, because by that time I had just about lost interest, and after that my father had to go out hunting and fishing alone. But on this spring day the weather had taken turns between sunshine and a light rain, and we caught more fish than we had ever caught before. I barely had time to get the line into the water before I could feel the tugging and pulling and out would come a fish big enough for a feast. The gars were jumping and making splashes all over the lake, and the turtles were diving off their logs, and the fish kept biting away. Clearly something was going on under there. Then the wind rose and the rain came down in heavy drops, and we paddled to land as fast as we could and made it to a deserted shack on Spit's land just in time. The drops made little clouds in the dust until the dust itself was wet and muddy, and the rain blew in gusts and rattled hard on the tin roof. We walked out again, and the whole earth was wet and cool: the trees heavy and glistening in the sun, and the rich delta land humming and making its grand noises. Then my father said, "We better be gettin' on back. If there're any fish left, we'll let 'em alone to grow."

15

I too was let alone to grow. One day when I was a much older boy, I left Yazoo on a bus, and I knew I would never return there to live again. I knew also that my boyhood was over.

Despite all the years that have passed, I can see the town now on some hot, still weekday afternoon in midsummer. Even the old red water truck is a diversion, coming slowly up Grand Avenue with its sprinklers on full force, the water making sizzling steam clouds on the pavement while half-naked children follow it up the street and play in the torrent until they are soaking wet. Over on Broadway, where the old men sit drowsily in straw chairs on the pavement near the Bon-Ton Cafe, little boys laze around on the sidewalk watching the big cars with out-of-state license plates whip by on the way to New Orleans or Memphis, the driver hardly knowing and certainly not caring what town this is. From way up on that fantastic hill, Broadway seems to end in a seething mist—little heat mirages that shimmer off the asphalt. On Main Street there is only a handful of cars parked here and there, and the merchants and lawyers sit in the shade under the broad awnings, talking slowly and aimlessly in the Southern summer way. Out by the River, the Clark Mansion is quiet and deserted and all the Yankee skeletons have been removed from its dark secret passages, and in the cemetery on the hill Ralph and Peewee and Honest Ed are eating moonpies near the witch's grave.

Although I now live hundreds of miles away from the old town, its streets and lanes are like a map on my consciousness, and the morning light reflects itself on the same fences and trees and fields of those driftless long-ago Saturdays. I feel, I could be right there now and grow up all over again. Then the 12 o'clock whistle at the sawmill sends out its loud bellow, echoing up the streets to the bend in the River, hardly making a ripple in the heavy indolence. My father is at the firehouse listening to the baseball game from New York, good old Skip is home dozing in the grass under his favorite elm tree, Spit McGee is trapping crawdads in the bayou. And Bubba, Muttonhead, Billy Rhodes, Henjie, and Big Boy? Right now they are probably gift wrapping a dead rat or roaming around in the red Model A, hot on the trail of lawbreakers.

Epilogue

So, David, I have told you what it was like for me when I was growing up. Although much would change, something there remained: some innocent quality that made possible, in the heart of a young and vulnerable boy, an allegiance and a love for one small place.

CPSIA information can be obtained
at www.ICGtesting.com
Printed in the USA
FFOW04n1845241014
8336FF